C000053414

# A New Life in
# New Zealand

This book is dedicated to
my wife Julie who pushes me when I need it
and is there for me at the end of the day.
To my children Zoë and Sam who brighten our every day
Without your support none of this would have been possible.

**howto**books

Please send for a free copy of our latest catalogue to:
3 Newtec Place, Magdalen Road
Oxford OX4 1RE, United Kingdom

info@howtobooks.co.uk
www.howtobooks.co.uk

# A New Life in New Zealand

JOIN PAUL GODDARD AND HIS FAMILY ON AN EMOTIONAL ROLLERCOASTER
AS THEY START LIFE AFRESH IN ANOTHER, BEAUTIFUL COUNTRY

## PAUL GODDARD

**howto**books

Published by
**How To Books Ltd,**
3 Newtec Place, Magdalen Road,
Oxford OX4 1RE. United Kingdom.
Tel: (01865) 793806. Fax: (01865) 248780
email: info@howtobooks.co.uk
www.howtobooks.co.uk

All rights reserved. No part of this work may be reproduced or stored in an information
retrieval system (other than for purposes of review) without the express permission of the
publisher in writing.

© Copyright 2004 Paul Goddard

**British Library Cataloguing in Publication Data.**
A catalogue record for this book is available from the British Library.

Photographs of the Goddard family by Vivien Edwards of Tauranga, New Zealand
Cover design by Baseline Arts Ltd, Oxford

Produced for How To Books by Deer Park Productions
Typeset and design by Baseline Arts Ltd, Oxford
Printed and bound in Great Britain

NOTE: The material contained in this book is set out in good faith for general guidance and no
liability can be accepted for loss or expense incurred as a result of relying in particular
circumstances on statements made in this book. Laws and regulations are complex and liable to
change, and readers should check the current position with the relevant authorities before
making personal arrangements.

# Contents

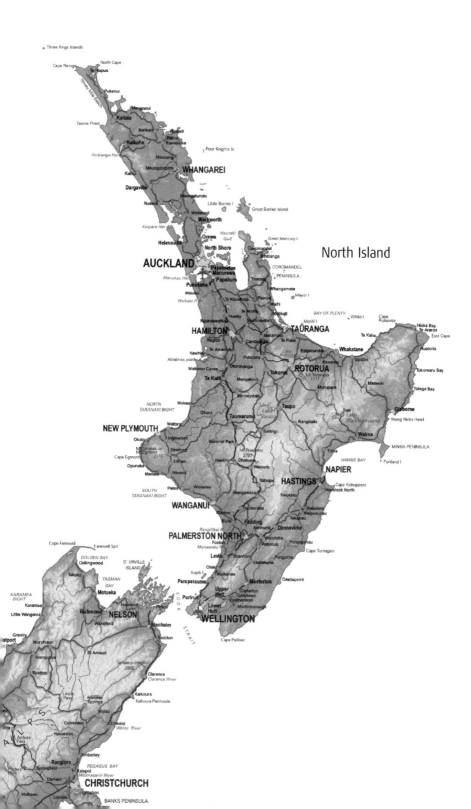

# New Zealand

## South Island

NORTH
TARANAKI BIGHT
Moka

NEW PLYMOUTH
Okato
Waitara
Inglewood
Mt Taranaki or
Mt Egmont
2518
Stratford
Cape Egmont
Eltham
Opunake
Manaia
Hawera
SOUTH
TARANAKI BIGHT
Pate
WAN

PALM

Cape Farewell
Farewell Spit
GOLDEN BAY
Collingwood
D'URVILLE
ISLAND
Takaka
TASMAN
BAY
Para
KARAMEA
BIGHT
Motueka
Co
O
K
Karamea
Havelock
Pe
Little Wanganui
Richmond
NELSON
Granity
Wakefield
Blenheim
Westport
Murchison
Seddon
Cape Foulwind
Inangahua
St Arnaud
Punakaiki
Reefton
Tapuae-o-Uenuku
2885
Clarence
Clarence River
Runanga
Lewis
Pass
Hanmer
Springs
Kaikoura
Greymouth
Kumara
Kaikoura Peninsula
Wairau
Hokitika
Otira
Culverden
Cheviot
Wairau River
Arthurs
Pass
Hawarden
Ross
Amberley
Harihari
Rangiora
PEGASUS BAY
Franz Josef Glacier/Waiau
Whataroa
Poters
Pass
Springfield
Kaiapoi
Waimakariri River
Fox Glacier
Darfield
CHRISTCHURCH
Aoraki/Mt Cook
3754
Lincoln
Mt Somers
Methven
Lyttelton
BANKS PENINSULA
Jackson Head
Aoraki/Mount Cook
Lake
Tekapo
Geraldine
Hinds
Akaroa
Ashburton
Rakaia River
Haast River/Haast
Haast
Lake
Pukaki
Fairlie
Temuka
Ashburton River/Hakatere
CANTERBURY BIGHT
Awarua Point
Haast Pass/
Tioritiri
Hari
Hari
Lake
Tekapo
Twizel
Rangitata River
Makarora
Timaru
Milford Sound/Piopiotahi
Mt Aspiring/Tititea
3027
Lake
Hawea
Lindis
Pass
Omarama
Milford
Sound
Wanaka
Waitaki River
Homer
Tunnel
Glenorchy
Tarras
Kurow
George Sound
Arrowtown
Waimate
Queenstown
Cromwell
Oamaru
Lake
Wakatipu
Ranfurly
Maheno
Doubtful Sound/Patea
Alexandra
Middlemarch
Hampden
Dagg Sound
Kingston
Palmerston
Te Anau
Roxburgh
Waikouaiti
Doubtful
Sound
Lake
Te Anau
Manapouri
Secretary I
Mossburn
Port Chalmers
Lake
Manapouri
Tapanui
Mosgiel
OTAGO PENINSULA
Dusky Sound
Ohai
Nightcaps
Lumsden
Lawrence
DUNEDIN
Winton
Gore
Clinton
Balclutha
Tuatapere
Mataura
Kaitangata
Clutha River
Riverton/Aparima
Edendale
Owaka
INVERCARGILL
FOVEAUX STRAIT
Bluff
Chaslands Mistake
Solander I
Ruapuke I
Codfish
Halfmoon
Bay (Oban)
Stewart Island/Rakiura
South Cape/Whiore

# Acknowledgements

**This past year has been an amazing ride for us – an adventure in every sense of the word. We have a few people to thank in enabling us to get this far.**

Firstly, our parents because without their support and encouragement I don't think we would have been able to even start out on our journey.

To the Brighter Pictures team especially Mellissa Porter, Ian Lilley, Jacquie Spector and also the behind the scenes crew for being so understanding.

In New Zealand, we would like to thank Priority One for their help on our arrival and continued support. Lorraine (and Dennis) from CAR CARE for going out of her way to help us succeed in our new business. The people on the Tauranga music scene, Glen, Tony and Benji at Brewers Bar, The team at Bay City music, Paul Cameron (keep Backbeat Rocking) and Derrin guitar maestro and book editor extraordinaire. The 'Rock' radio station for keeping us sane and happy. To the friends we've made and are still to make and finally to The Emigration Group for taking the stress out of making the move and their continued support of our new life here.

How To books, thanks for getting this book out so quickly and for all your support.

After reading this book you may or may not decide to emigrate. I just hope we have shown that if you have determination, drive and support you can achieve anything.

**Paul Goddard**

## PUBLISHER'S ACKNOWLEDGEMENTS

How To Books would like to thank Vivien Edwards of Tauranga, New Zealand for her photographs of the Goddard family, together with the following photographs:

Autumn leaves, McLarens Falls Park
Boats, Tauranga Rail Bridge
Café culture in mall, Tauranga
Mt Hytt, Rakaia Gorge
Sail Away concert Tuapiro Point, Upper Tauranga Harbour
Southern Alps
Statue of Wairaka on the rock at the Whakatane River
Surf on rocks and gnarled pohutakawas, Mauao base track
View from Plummers Point towards the end of Te Puna Peninsula
Waikato River, Hamilton

Thanks also to Bay of Plenty Tourism for the following photographs:
Mount Maunganui Beach
Sailing in Tauranga Harbour
Tauranga Harbour Bridge

All other photographs in the book are courtesy of Tourism New Zealand.

# Introduction

**There are so many books written about emigrating that the facts and figures are there for anyone to find, should they choose to look – and using the internet to do research is making the process of emigrating even easier. In fact, it makes you wonder how people ever emigrated before the internet existed.**

I know if the company I had been working for prior to our emigration had ever found out just how much of their time I spent doing my research then we may have been moving much sooner than initially planned.

Given that all the relevant facts and figures are already out there, the idea of this particular book is not to duplicate what is already available, but to add to it by showing, on a personal note, what it is really like to leave family and friends behind and set up a new life in New Zealand.

The interesting, and vital, nuts-and-bolts facts and figures of living here in New Zealand – i.e. the relative cost of a loaf of bread, etc. – can be found on the internet, and to that end there is a list of useful websites and contacts at the end of this book – along with numerous hints and tips throughout the book to help with the process of emigrating. What you won't find on the internet, however, and what we want to show, is what you really go through as a family: the day-to-day things that will either bring you closer together or drive you apart.

All in all, it has been an amazing ride so far – as you may have already seen in the TV programme *Get a New Life* – and in our short time here in New Zealand we have certainly had our share of highs and lows. Thanks, mainly, to the programme's publicity of our self-inflicted plight, from the start we have been inundated with emails and visits from people looking at making the move out here. Consequently, many of the observations and much of the advice that we share in this book, is drawn from that correspondence and those meetings.

In helping others who are contemplating a move far from home, we have learned a lot about what we have actually been through ourselves, what we have achieved and how our advice might influence or help others. In that spirit, what follows will hopefully offer more people the kind of advice we would have found invaluable.

Fortunately, one of the things we did understand correctly right from the start was the importance of research. We did a huge amount of research before the move, and anybody seriously considering emigrating must similarly do as much research as possible to have even a fighting chance of coming to grips with the many challenges that emigration throws up.

However, as alluded to above, no amount of research can possibly tell you everything there is to learn about the day-to-day reality of actually living in your newly chosen country: there are certain things you will only find out once you live there. And, again, that is why we have written this book.

For those of you considering emigrating we feel it is important we give a balanced viewpoint throughout the book: for us there have been highs, and there have been lows, and I hope we are able to convey these equally and accurately in context.

To give you a bit of background, we came out to New Zealand (or Aotearoa, 'the land of the long white cloud') for, amongst others, the following reasons:

■ the friendly people
■ the low crime rate
■ it's a great place to bring up children
■ the lifestyle.

So is New Zealand life, as they say here, 'sweet as'?

Read on...

A quick visit to The Emigration Group in Chester confirmed that we would indeed meet the requirements of the long-term business visa, and hence get into New Zealand, by buying a Car Care franchise. So, just as we had done earlier with the rehearsal studio, we made an on-the-spot decision and took the plunge, putting the house up for sale, selling the studio and applying for our visa.

Naturally, research fanatics that we were, a visit to New Zealand was warranted, so we booked a two-week holiday-cum-fact-finding mission to Auckland and Tauranga.

As an aside, people always ask me why we chose Tauranga as a place to consider settling in – many Kiwis among them. Well, it happened like this: I was doing my usual (paid) internet research when a map of New Zealand appeared, and on it was an area called the Bay of Plenty. I figured it must have been given such a glowing title for a good reason – and it certainly appealed more than the less attractively named Poverty Bay not far to the east on the map – so I looked a bit closer.

As I quickly learned, Tauranga is the main city in the Bay of Plenty – the Bay, to the locals – and is a stunning place to look at, especially via the internet in a cold factory on a bleak Saturday morning in Coventry. At first glance, Tauranga seemed to have everything we were looking for: a beach lifestyle, but with a touch of the city life we were used to.

I saved a picture of Tauranga's landmark Mount Maunganui (an amazing extinct volcano which sits at the end of the main beach in Tauranga) as wallpaper on my desktop computer and told everybody who came into my office, 'That's where I'm going to live'. Every day from then on was spent planning the move; our impending emigration completely took over our lives.

Looking back, in my enthusiasm I must have bored and/or infuriated more than a few people with my third-hand tales of New Zealand, gleaned from the latest migration book or from 'British xpats' websites. But I sincerely believe there is nothing worse than regret, and that if you are comitting to doing anything in life you should go for it 100 per cent. So I like to think that my unbridled enthusiasm also had a positive effect on those around me.

## OUR RESEARCH VISIT

The two-week research visit to New Zealand was booked for October and I remember getting on the plane and saying to Julie, 'I hope we like this place because in three months we could be living there'.

From the UK to New Zealand is a hell of a flight – even with children like ours who love flying – but it gives you plenty of time to think about what you are really doing, and to read the latest New Zealand travel guide (the research never stops!).

We flew via LA and had a break there, and I definitely recommend this to anyone making the journey as a great way to break up the long haul.

## ROSE TINTED GLASSES

When you fly to New Zealand via the United States you get a real sense of how far away from the rest of the world you really are heading. You fly over the pacific for what seems like an eternity without seeing land, and then just when you've given up all hope of ever touching down on terra firma again, all of a sudden there are lush green fields everywhere.

My first clear memory of landing in New Zealand was that the air was crisp and fresh. In fact, it reminded me a lot of a visit we had made to the Shetland Islands, though needless to say, the climate here in the South Pacific was a bit warmer.

Sensibly, we had decided to book a few days' accommodation in Auckland to get over the jet lag, and we also planned to use some of that time to meet with our main Kiwi contact, Lorraine, who owned the NZ Car Care master franchise. We had been comunicating with Lorraine via the internet for quite a while so Julie and I were quite excited to be finally meeting her – not to mention a little apprehensive about the business we were already half committed to buying.

Thankfully, the first meeting went well and Lorraine had helped greatly in putting together the requisite business plan for our subsequent dealings with New Zealand Immigration. This is one of the advantages of buying a franchise: it is an established business idea, and facts and figures are readily available. We discussed all the options and were offered the choice of a franchise in Tauranga or Auckland.

## A TASTE OF AUCKLAND

To put you in the picture, Auckland is a beautiful city. It has a population of around one million, widely spread, and is home to most of the country's big businesses, and to the main sporting venues and theatres.

The Americas Cup was on when we arrived so the harbour was a hive of activity. The city seemed busy but had a more laid back feel than somewhere like London (maybe it was just the jet lag). The 328-metre high Sky Tower dominates the skyline, but apart from this, high-rises are relatively few and far between, and not on the scale of most other cities of similar size.

We relaxed a little in Auckland, browsing the shops and taking in some of the sites. I suppose, subconsciously at least, we had already chosen Tauranga as the place we wanted to settle – even though we had never been there – so the few days we had in Auckland we spent as tourists. After all, big city life – even on this clearly more manageable scale – was one of the things we were trying to get away from and although it would have been easier to get the business off the ground in Auckland, with the higher population, we wanted a more laid-back beach lifestyle so stuck to our guns.

## HEADING EAST

We left our motel (rather quickly after Julie had her first encounter with a rather large New Zealand cockroach) and set off on the three-hour drive east to Tauranga and the Bay of Plenty. Once out of Auckland, State Highway 2 quickly thins out, and looking at the sparsely populated landscape and the near empty roads I can remember thinking we were in the Wild West of America. In fact, you notice the influence America has on New Zealand in many ways, more of which I will explain later in the book. Throughout the drive the land was flat, with wooden farmhouses and horses and cattle on either side.

The next piece of scenery we encountered, however, was pure NZ. The Kaimais are a mountain range that runs along the spine of the North Island, and the drive through the Karangahake Gorge, which bisects the range, is spectacular. A narrow, twisting road runs through the gorge, where the beauty and power of the river's rushing water is set against the imposing presence of the tree- and fern-covered jagged rockface that towers either side of you. Personally, I have a theory that scenery like this is one of the reasons New Zealand has such a high death rate on its roads. Julie was constantly telling me to keep my eyes on the road as I negotiated the turns while trying to figure out what speed 60 km/h is meant to be.

Having successfully negotiated the Gorge, the next thing that lets you know you have arrived in the Bay of Plenty is the sea! Julie had lived by the sea in the Shetland isles but it was new to me and the kids, and was definitely one of the reasons I wanted to emigrate. I have always been drawn to it and always wanted to retire by the sea, but let's face it, the English sea side can be pretty cold, polluted and uninviting, so the smiles on Zoë and Sam's faces said it all.

TAURANGA HERE WE COME!

## TAURANGA – SOME BASIC FACTS

I'll take a break from the narrative here to give you a few facts about Tauranga.

The three main areas are Tauranga centre, Papamoa (the fastest growing area in 2002) and Mount Maunganui, affectionately called 'the Mount' ('the Bay', 'the Mount'... you get the picture). The latter, the beach peninsula capped by Mount Maunganui itself, is an amazing feature and must lure new migrants and visitors like the sirens in old sea folklore. Remember, it is the image of Mount Maunganui that had kept me going on those cold Saturday mornings at work in the UK.

The population of Tauranga is around 140,000 but it is growing at a rate of around 4 per cent or 100 people per week, making it officially (September 2003) New Zealand's fastest growing city. New houses are springing up everywhere, but the area remains visually stunning. House prices are booming, with property in the Mount and Papamoa regions having risen in value by 20 per cent in 2002. Around 44 per cent of New Zealand's population live within 200 kilometres of the Bay of Plenty region.

At its present rate of growth, Tauranga will soon be New Zealand's fourth largest city, and it continues to be the place most New Zealanders would like to live. As an added bonus, for family-minded people such as ourselves, some of the best schools and colleges in New Zealand are located here and secondary results are above the national average.

This talk of rapid growth and housing booms shouldn't put you off, however, if you are looking for a quieter lifestyle, as Tauranga still has a small town feel to it, and it seems that the developers are taking care to ensure that Tauranga doesn't turn into the kind of concrete jungle we are used to in the UK.

As far as climate goes, here in Tauranga we get 2200–2400 hours of sunshine per year, with an average summer temperature of 24° Celsius, and a very bearable winter average of 15°. The outdoor lifestyle is as least as big here as in the rest of New Zealand so you can take your pick from fishing, surfing, boating, walking, swimming (with or without dolphins) or you can watch mighty White Island (New Zealand's only active marine volcano) erupting on a clear day. Perhaps now you can see some of the reasons why we wanted to set up home here!

**FIRST IMPRESSIONS**

Anyway, back to that initial journey eastward from Auckland to what would eventually prove to be our new home.

Having arrived in Tauranga, we booked into a motor lodge and decided to explore. The first thing that amazed us was the fact that most children – not to mention quite a few adults – weren't wearing any shoes! As we were to learn, walking on concrete in the rain, in supermarkets, cinemas… a lot of people here just don't wear shoes in the summer (of course, our own kids are now running around shoeless). I commented on how they can't have much of a problem with dog mess around here!

With time limited, we didn't want to treat the remaining ten days left as a holiday and decided to cram in as much research as possible. First on the list, food.

## Food

Julie is a vegetarian and so the supermarkets were top of our list. Countdown and Woolworth's are the two main supermarkets (scarily, both owned by the same parent company) and although not up to the standards of Sainsbury's at home, they are good.

If you happen to be vegetarian, however, be warned: most food will not have the friendly 'V' sign and this means checking the ingredients on the back. Add to this the fact that a lot of chips in the takeaways are still cooked in beef fat – although the switch to vegetable oil does seem to be happening. I think people in New Zealand are becoming more aware that not everyone eats animal products but it is definitely behind the UK in these terms.

## Education

Settling the children into a new lifestyle in a strange country was obviously going to be a major concern for us, especially with a ten-year-old Zoë, so our next focus was on education. Zoë's main concern was settling into a new school, and all that this entails, so we spent a lot of time visiting various schools in the area.

Some schools had waiting lists and some appeared markedly better than others, but in the end we decided to let Zoë have the final choice as she would be going into primary for one year before changing to intermediate. Our reckoning behind this was that if the primary school she chose was not up to the standard we were after then we could always change to something more suitable when she moved to intermediate.

Schools in New Zealand run differently to British ones, with children starting at primary level then generally moving to an intermediate school at 11 for two years before going on to high school.

After careful consideration, Zoë chose Mount Maunganui Primary School, which suited us perfectly because we didn't need to be in the catchment area to enrol there, and as yet we had no idea where we would be living. The staff were very helpful and let us enrol Zoë even though we didn't have a firm arrival date, and this definitely put Zoë's mind at ease.

If anyone is considering taking children of school age to a new country I would thoroughly recommend taking them with you on your fact-finding holiday.

**Housing**

Another major concern, and attraction, was housing. Much has been written elsewhere about houses in New Zealand compared with the UK and I have to admit this was a big factor in our move here. In the UK we lived in a nice new three-bedroom detached house next to a golf course and canal. However after driving around Papamoa looking at the showhomes we couldn't believe what we could get for the equivalent money here.

Papamoa is developing fast and most of the houses are under four years old. We saw homes with stereo systems built into the walls, central vacuuming – which is a powerful vacuum built into the garage that allows you to simply plug a hose into sockets conveniently located in each room – and outdoor spa and swimming pools.

Huge double garages are a big plus, usually with a direct entrance into the house so you won't get wet running from the car to the front door when it's raining.

The size of these new houses is also a big draw, especially when you have children and pets. My advice is to beware as some estate agents will try to get you to put a deposit (non-refundable) on a house even though you haven't got your permanent residence visa yet. I must admit, some of the houses are so nice that you could almost be forgiven for feeling tempted to hand over the deposit on the spot.

## TAKING THE PLUNGE

Having satisfied ourselves about the important things – food, schools and housing – and having liked what we had seen of Tauranga and its surrounds, we decided to take the risk of starting our proposed Car Care franchise in Tauranga. We felt the place would offer us the lifestyle we were looking for, and although we knew we would have the struggle of setting up a new business, we felt it would be worth the risk and effort.

So we drove back to Lorraine in Auckland and paid a refundable deposit on the business. We had been told that long-term business visas were taking around three months to process so we hoped to be back out for January or February.

At that stage, with our research trip over, we headed home to the UK, and I don't think we had any doubts about what we were trying to do. We had even noted with glee how we hadn't seen any car washes on the garages in Tauranga, so we expected the car grooming business to do well. Of course, this is an example of seeing the world through 'rose tinted glasses' as there are car washes and car valet firms all over Tauranga, but in some respects we were only looking for what we wanted to see.

## BACK IN ENGLAND

We arrived back to a rainy UK and spent the next few weeks organising removal people and checking the internet every day to see if our visas had been granted. As we had already sold our rehearsal studio, we realised money was only going to get tighter and tighter the longer we stayed in the UK.

Try to imagine my disappointment, then, when a phone call to New Zealand Immigration to check on the progress of our visa resulted in us being informed that visas were now taking six to nine months to process! (Apparently this longer backlog was down to a change in accountancy firms used to check applicants' business plans.)

At this stage, I must admit I didn't know what to do. Lorraine, from Car Care NZ, had taken out a *Yellow Pages* advertisement in the Tauranga edition and orders for work were already starting to come in. Meanwhile, in the UK, with no income, our mortgage was starting to drain our funds, and Christmas was looming large on the horizon.

It was around this time that I came across the 'British xpats' website (www.britishexpats.com). It is a really helpful site, wherever you are looking at emigrating, and you can even talk to people who have already made the move before you.

The BBC started a thread on this site asking people who were looking at emigrating in the coming months to get in touch, as they were producing a TV programme on the subject. I sent an email, then a home video that they asked for, and Julie and I answered a few questions from a researcher who visited us. We told her about the delay in our visa applications and when she left Julie said, 'well, we're not going to be involved in that then'.

## GOOD NEWS

Two days later I was at work early, diligently checking my emails as usual, and the message we had been waiting for finally arrived. Our visas had been granted! I remember running around work with a copy of the email.

It was a good day and a huge weight off our minds.

The thing with the BBC was strange as I had no doubt that they would use us for the programme even though at this stage we were none the wiser as to what it was. Still, the fact our visas had been granted was a good omen, and I had a gut feeling there was more good news to come. Julie was completely the opposite, however, and wasn't even sure if she wanted us to show ourselves going through what was bound to be a stressful time.

With the BBC avenue still up in the air, we concentrated on making the most of what could be our last Christmas in the UK.

Relatives were due to stay with us over Christmas and generally people were wishing us luck and saying how they wished they had the opportunity to emigrate. In fact I can honestly say we never had one person ask us why we wanted to leave, which did surprise me – after all, we had good jobs and a nice house, etc.

Then out of the blue we had a phone call saying that the producer of the BBC programme wanted to come and ask us a few more questions and would the 23rd of December be OK. She was due to arrive at 11 a.m. and we were all inside watching TV when the doorbell rang. I was horrified to see about eight people on our drive with TV cameras and lights!

The rest of the day just turned into a blur as we rapidly tried to come to terms with the fact that we had indeed been chosen to be featured by the BBC.

## LAST-MINUTE PREPARATIONS

Everything was suddenly happening so fast. The BBC notified us that they had flights booked for us on the 18th of January, and this only gave us a couple of weeks to organise everything. In shock, we actually phoned them the next day to say we had changed our minds and couldn't do it as it was too soon. Obviously empathetic to our state of panic, they offered to help and so with this assurance, and with the initial panic subsiding, we set our minds to actually completing what we had been preparing for.

The removal company was booked. We used John Masons, who had been recommended via the 'British xpats' website, and they were excellent. The mortgage on the house was deferred for three months, just in case it didn't sell. Then we settled down – if 'settled' is the correct word to us in the face of such turmoil – to a very strange Christmas.

The stress levels were rising but I think the fact that we had such a significant diversion as Christmas in the way helped take our minds off things for a while. The speed at which things were now moving was obviously a shock to everybody, not least of all our parents, who had expected to have us around a little while longer. And the guilt of taking their grandchildren away from them was beginning to sink in with us.

At first, having a film crew around felt strange, but in a way it made what we were doing seem a little less real, and in that sense perhaps helped alleviate some of the stress rather than exacerbate it. In no time at all we got used to the cameras being around, though it has to be said that there were times – especially when we were saying goodbye to people we would probably never see again – when having a camera around took away some of the intimacy of the moment.

## SAYING GOODBYE

There was so much to arrange, and in such a short time. Fortunately, organisation had always been Julie's forte, so we soon had all the loose ends tied up. Pretty soon, all that remained to organise was our leaving party. Did I say 'party'? I meant 'parties': we actually ended up having three, and we enjoyed them all immensely.

The first party was way back in October when we sold the rehearsal studio, and this was one of the best nights I've ever had, with all the local bands there. In a true *Blues Brothers* moment I even reformed 'the band' – my first band – for a one-off farewell performance. We were well respected in the music scene and I wondered if we would achieve anything like this in New Zealand.

The next party was at my mum and dad's local on a Saturday night. Then we ended up having another party at the same pub on the following Wednesday to cater for the people who hadn't been able to make the Saturday one.

Strangely, it was during these party nights that I experienced my first doubts about what we were embarking upon. We had a lot of friends and close family and these semi-official farewells brought home to us just what we would be leaving behind. It was strange, and hard, to think that we might never see some of these people again, so there were a lot of tears mixed in with the laughter.

Our own families were coping as best they could, in their own ways, with the prospect of our rapidly approaching departure, though Julie's mum took it very hard. We insisted that we didn't want any of the family coming to see us off at the airport, as it would have just been too traumatic for everybody. As it was, I know when Julie reads this the memories will come back and the tears will flow again.

Finally saying goodbye to our families, at that stage, has been the hardest thing about emigrating so far away and I would never want to go through it again. In all honesty, we had to stop the car after we had set off for the airport from my parent's house as we were all in such a state and I couldn't see where I was driving!

It was an eerie, quiet, lonely drive down to London with the whole family thinking about what we were each leaving behind. Thankfully, once we reached the airport we had the film crew to take our mind off things.

Once we were well and truly on our way, as the plane flew over America, I had what I can only describe as a mild panic attack. I was looking out of the window and it all just hit me like a ton of bricks: 'what the hell are we doing?!' It was as if my life up to that point had flashed before me and I couldn't see what was coming next.

At that moment I had never felt so alone or with such a weight on my shoulders. The questions wouldn't stop: What would the business be like? Would it work? Would we get through this as a family or could it drive us apart? I turned from the window and saw Zoë and Sam watching TV with the headphones on and Julie buried in a book and as suddenly as the panic had come, it was gone.

## WELCOME TO NEW ZEALAND

This time arriving in NZ felt different.

For me, more than any romantic image of arrival, it was now simply about survival. We had put everything into setting up a new business and I knew the funds we had brought over wouldn't last indefinitely. I needed to get started, immediately, on building a new business and income that would support us in our new life. So, two days after arriving in our adopted country, I was out being trained in my new business.

One advantage of buying a franchise is the master franchisee (owner of the franchise) should guide you through the whole process of being self-employed in the new country. Laws effecting tax and business are much the same in New Zealand as in the UK, so the first thing I had to do was get my IRD number (a bit like national insurance number) and register for GST (VAT). I found the Inland Revenue people very helpful and it was quite a simple process.

## SORTING OUT THE BASICS

Three days later, now pretty thoroughly versed in the ways of Car Care, we were on our way to Tauranga to begin our new life in a rental house that the BBC had helped tie up for us.

The weather was fantastic, but we immediately noticed more flies and insects than on our previous visit. In fact, the situation was so bad that we couldn't leave windows open in the house, so it became more like an oven than a home. There were spiders everywhere, and even though we were told that none were poisonous we soon found out from a neighbour that the white tip can give a nasty bite!

As our belongings wouldn't be arriving for another couple of months the first thing we needed was furniture. This was where we had our first experience of that famed New Zealand friendliness.

We had purchased a fridge freezer from Farmers department store (sort of like a small version of Alders or Debenhams in the UK) and went into a nearby furniture shop called Simply Furniture. There we wanted to purchase a lounge suite and dining table with chairs made from RIMU wood – which is basically recycled floorboards, complete with nail holes for that added character. We also needed a bed, but didn't want to buy one as ours was on its way here. What happened next certainly wouldn't have happened in Coventry.

The guy from Simply Furniture said we could hire a brand new bed from him until ours arrived. That was a fantastic deal, but we had just paid for the freezer and had reached the daily limit on our new cashpoint card, so feared we wouldn't be able to take him up on his generous offer. Not to worry, the very nice store owner loaded all the stuff we wanted into his van, gave me the keys and said, 'Pick up your freezer from Farmers, take all the stuff home, pay me when you can... Oh, and by the way, I'm going home now so just drop the van off at the back of the shop when you've finished with it.'

We couldn't believe it! We had just arrived in the country and this guy was trusting us with his stock and his van – and we didn't even have the film crew with us.

Now, I think people are all different and for every good person there's probably a bad one, but I would say generally New Zealanders are friendlier than people in the UK. I know that's a huge generalisation, but it's something I've observed personally. It may have something to do with the more relaxed lifestyle and attitudes here, which in turn has everything to do with a smaller population.

The UK is overcrowded, and when you've lived in that kind of situation you immediately become very aware of the space around you in New Zealand: from the large houses to the miles of uncrowded beaches to the small, uncrowded schools. It all has a very subtle effect and people appear, generally, less 'wound up'.

## GETTING THE BUSINESS STARTED

Back to the story. We now had a home and some furniture – the next step was to get the business up and running. We knew it would be hard but after looking at all the cars and boats around we did expect to be very busy very quickly. New Zealand is only second behind California in car ownership figures per capita.

One thing we hadn't figured on, though, was the competition from the fixed valet sites. We had never seen so many used car yards in our life for such a small town and assumed this would be our main source of income. However, it soon became apparent that these were all being catered for by the fixed sites. Work did start to come in, but it was a lot slower than we had hoped. Still, it was early days so we weren't overly worried.

The work was physically demanding but I was enjoying being out in the sunshine and working in a different place every day. Working in a factory in the UK can become very monotonous, so this was a nice change. When I wasn't actually grooming vehicles, we would all go out and drop flyers advertising the business. Our attitude was, and still is, that we work 9 to 5 Monday to Friday even if we aren't actually grooming cars all this time.

## SAM HAS AN ACCIDENT

After a few days in Tauranga I had to go back up to Auckland to have some further Car Care training. It was the first time Julie and I had spent any real time apart for years and I wasn't too happy about leaving her so soon into our new life. But needs must, so off to Auckland I went.

Training went well but on the first evening I had a phone call from Julie saying that Sam had fallen off his new bike and hurt his arm. She had spent hours at the hospital and his arm had been put in plaster. I really wanted to come back and be with them all but I couldn't and was very glad the BBC crew were there with her.

When I returned, Sam looked very sorry for himself and Julie was quite down. It hit home to me that it's at times like these that you really miss having family around. Suddenly, a simple thing like being able to pop around to your parents' for a cup of tea – which we had always taken for granted – shoots to the top of your wish-list and homesickness begins to rear its ugly head.

At home, the heat in the rental house was becoming a problem. We bought some fans, though it could still prove to be quite unbearable at night. The insects were beginning to annoy us a bit as well. We were constantly picking up spiders and grasshoppers and all sorts of other creepy crawlies and there seemed to be a constant stream of flies. The reason for this soon became apparent when Julie went to hang out the washing one morning. Peering over the back fence at her was a herd of cows complete with a cloud of flies buzzing around their heads.

We decided we needed to look at somewhere else to live as soon as we could. Also, our dogs were due to arrive soon from the UK and pets were not allowed.

### TIME TO MOVE

While I groomed cars and dropped Car Care flyers around town, Julie decided to look at houses. Rental property in Tauranga is very hard to come across, especially in summer when it seems that all the Kiwis who haven't already moved to the area decide to visit for their summer holidays. So we decided to look at a rent-to-buy agreement on a property an estate agent we had initially found over the internet had highlighted for us.

'Rent-to-buy' basically entails paying a deposit on the property and then setting a date by which the purchase will be completed – in the meantime you pay rent on the property.

This seemed perfect for us in our current situation as we had the upcoming problem with the dogs arriving, and our house in the UK hadn't sold so we couldn't contemplate getting a mortgage here yet. We also wanted to settle the children as quickly as possible, so a rent-to-buy option would remove any potential risk of having to move from rental to rental.

Having gone to look at the house our estate agent had recommended, Julie called me on the mobile to come and look at the property for myself, and she was very excited. The house seemed massive, and seemed incredibly reasonably priced at $305,000! (By this time we had looked at a lot of properties in the $300,000 price range and this house seemed like a bargain.)

The house had a large drive and front garden, a big double garage and was on a larger than average plot (770 sq.m). The four bedrooms were more than we needed but we knew the extra bedroom would come in handy as an office, and as a spare bedroom for when relatives visited. We also found out that the builder of the property had a very good reputation and had put a lot of extras into the finish of the house.

The location was also great, with just a ten-minute walk to the beach, and five minutes to the nearest shopping plaza, so we knew we had to act immediately. An agreement was drawn up the next day setting the selling price at $305,000 and the rent at $300 per week. We only had to put a $5000 deposit down and had a year to sell the house in the UK.

The agreement was signed and we couldn't wait to move in.

The pressure was now really on for me to start finding bookings for the business, so I was keen to meet as many prospective customers as possible. Then out of the blue we had a phone call from a company called Priority One, whom NZ Immigration had advised of our arrival.

Priority One are set up to encourage and help business people relocate to Tauranga by offering them help, advice and useful contacts, and with 'useful contacts' at the top of my shopping list I thought this would be an excellent opportunity to further our business prospects.

## NETWORKING, NEW ZEALAND STYLE

We met with the Priority One team and they were very helpful. After some initial discussions, they invited us out on a boat they had chartered for the Around Alone yacht race (as the name suggest, a solo global circumnavigation race), which was leaving Tauranga that coming weekend. I knew that this would be an ideal networking opportunity for us as a lot of successful local businesspeople would also be on the boat.

The day of the race was amazing. We were out at sea surrounded by hundreds of boats, jet skis and even helicopters. The people from Priority One were introducing us to everyone who was anyone in Tauranga and we felt happy that we were really going to get somewhere in our new venture. But the biggest surprise was yet to come.

When we arrived back on land we were asked if we would like to meet the Prime Minister of New Zealand, Helen Clarke. This was a massive shock for us and the film crew. We needn't have been nervous though as this was meeting the Prime Minister 'New Zealand style'.

Helen Clarke was enjoying lunch at Spinnakers, a very nice restaurant on the harbourside, and we really didn't know what to expect as we walked into the building. I can remember wondering where all the security guards were and thinking there would be no way we would actually get close enough to talk to her. Trying to keep out of trouble, and to look as inconspicuous as you can with a camera crew in tow, we helped ourselves to champagne and mingled with a few of the people we had met on the boat.

I couldn't believe how informal everything was. Most people were dressed in shorts and T-shirts and the Prime Minister was just mingling with guests like everybody else. If this had been the UK we would probably have had to pay for tickets, worn a bow tie and if we were really lucky we may have got a signed photograph of Tony Blair.

Well, this is New Zealand and the PM was introduced to us by the people from Priority One. We settled down to a very interesting conversation that varied from immigration to dog control laws to the New Zealand music scene. During this 20-minute chat Helen Clarke was very impressive in her knowledge on all subjects.

## SAM HAS ANOTHER ACCIDENT!

Then Sam had another one of his little accidents! The Prime Minister was giving a speech about the Around Alone race when Zoë managed to stand on Sam's remaining 'good' arm. There was a high-pitched scream and everyone, including the PM, looked around. We took Sam outside to calm him down and to look at his arm.

We had seen him like this before and as there were no marks and he could move it we decided to take him home and keep an eye on it. The next morning, however, he still wouldn't move his arm properly so we drove him down to the hospital again.

The service at the hospital was excellent once again. They took X-ray after X-ray, consulted amongst each other and generally spent a lot of time with us, even though the accident and emergency department is always very busy. Even though – like the other arm – this one wasn't broken, they decided to put it in plaster, mainly as a precaution and to rest any damage that may have been done. We had only been in the country three weeks and Sam had temporarily lost the use of both arms!

However, generally speaking, things were going well. On the domestic front, with a deposit on a new house, we were settling in fast. On the business side, things were slow but building and we were enjoying the summer weather. We weren't about to fall into the trap of 'all work and no play', however, so we decided to try out some of the New Zealand lifestyle that we had come here for.

## THE GREAT OUTDOORS

Living by the sea had a massive appeal to me and I always envisaged retiring to the coast in some exotic location. I'm 34 years old so moving to Tauranga meant it felt like my dream had come true way ahead of time.

The beaches in Tauranga are amazing: miles of golden sand, stunning views and plenty of room even in the summer. Zoë and I decided to try our hand at surfing and took a one-hour beginners lesson. After about ten minutes of falling off and getting used to the salt stinging my eyes I was hooked.

If you have never tried surfing and get the opportunity, then do so, because even though surfing is ridiculously difficult and you leave the water completely shattered, all other extraneous thoughts leave your mind, making it a great stress-beater. I'd have bought a surfboard there and then but we knew money would get tight soon if the house in the UK didn't sell, so my new hobby would have to wait.

We also thought it was about time that we took a walk up the Mount. We set off on what is about a 40-minute trek up this amazing extinct volcano. From the top the views were amazing, and this walk has become one of our favourite pastimes on a Sunday afternoon.

The number of outdoor activities readily available around here is almost endless: boating, fishing, beach volleyball, kite surfing, blokarting, skydiving, gliding – in fact if it doesn't exist then you can't help feeling that the Kiwis will invent it.

Most of the world's dangerous sports were invented in New Zealand and you have to wonder why people who live in such a beautiful place would dream up so many ways to potentially kill themselves. I must admit, though, that I can't wait to experience some of these extreme sports myself.

## TRYING THE NIGHTLIFE

Even in scenic New Zealand, however, not all activity is limited to the outdoors, so we decided to check out a local band at a place called the Office Bar. This was our first proper night out since we arrived and we used a babysitting service which had been recommended to us.

Now if you do make the move out here, be warned: the babysitter and the taxi will be the most expensive part of your evening out. The babysitter charges $10 per hour and a taxi ride from where we live to the mount (around 12 km) costs around $20 one way, so an average night out will cost around $100 before you've even bought a drink! Children here have to be 15 before they can be left alone to look after their sibling so I don't think we'll be having as many nights out as we did in the UK.

Babysitters and taxis aside, though, the Office Bar was fantastic. The band was loud, it was a warm summer evening and we were meeting people our own age for the first time. I did get a bit homesick, though, thinking about all the bands we used to see back home and wondering what they were up to.

We got talking to some of the band members afterwards and told them about our rehearsal studio in the UK. They practically begged us to set up something similar here as there is nowhere for bands to rehearse, but the long hours associated with the rehearsal studio were something we had come to New Zealand to get away from and so we left happy that we had at least found a vibrant music scene.

One of the reasons that this night out had been the first chance for us to meet people our own age is that Tauranga has a massive retirement population. It is cheekily referred to by the younger people as 'God's waiting room' or the place of 'the newly weds and the nearly deads', and struggles to shake off its long-held image as a retirement village by the sea. Paradoxically, it is also one of the most popular places for young people to come for the holidays, with excellent nightlife, bars, restaurants, cafes, etc.

On the BBC front, our first set of filming was now coming to an end, and to round things off the crew treated us to a meal out. We felt confident that we had everything in place to start our new life, but over the past two months – and especially since arriving in New Zealand – the crew had become our surrogate family. There were lots of tears at the end of an excellent night and as they walked away I can honestly say we had never felt so alone. It was a scary feeling; having them around had probably delayed the feelings that were to come. As we were to learn, our struggle had just begun…

Chapter Two

# It's a Long Way Home

**Although it was the middle of summer, the day after the film crew left it started to rain and rain and rain... In fact it rained solidly for over a week. I had no bookings for Car Care and another factor that I hadn't considered in our move was how the weather would affect my income.**

It's not that I can't work in the rain but that people don't want their cars grooming when the weather is so bad. We were feeling low anyway after the crew had gone and this just felt like a really bad omen. Homesickness hit Julie and the fact that the house in the UK looked no nearer to selling was also putting a strain on us.

## TRYING TO SELL OUR HOUSE

We decided to try a new estate agent and phoned Connells as they had been recommended to us. The fees they quoted were a lot higher than other agents but we decided to go with them as long as they kept us informed as to what was happening.

Now the best advice I can give to anybody considering emigrating is SELL YOUR HOUSE FIRST!

This has been the biggest nightmare our whole time out here. We had a new three-bedroom detached house in a nice area and yet it took ten months to sell our property in the UK.

We had to borrow money from a friend just to be able to stay in New Zealand as our funds had run out and the banks here can't help you if you don't have any assets here. Then to top it all when the house eventually did sell the estate agent charged us higher fees than we were quoted.

So if you do leave your house unsold make sure all relevant documents are sent to you to sign and not to family members back home.

## SETTLING IN AT SCHOOL

So the pressure on us was slowly building and homesickness was really getting to Julie. The only real positive factor in all this time was the kids were loving it here. Zoë really settled in at her school and we had started Sam at a local nursery so that Julie could come out to work with me. One reason we chose Tauranga was the fact that it has some of the best schools in New Zealand and school life here is certainly different to the UK.

The school year rather sensibly runs from January to December but it is in the classroom that you really notice the difference.

Julie was invited to a parents day at Zoë's school, but this wasn't the usual five-minute chat with a teacher that we used to get in Coventry. Julie could spend the whole day sitting in on Zoë's class, so she had a rather interesting afternoon and even took Sam along.

The first thing Julie noticed was the relaxed teaching style. The classroom organisation actually appeared quite chaotic at first but it soon became apparent that the children all knew what they were supposed to be doing and the teacher had total control. Sam was allowed to join in on the art session and proceeded to splash paint everywhere (well having both arms in plaster isn't very conducive to creating a masterpiece).

There have been lots of differences we have noticed in the New Zealand style of schooling and at another parents evening (BBQ and drinks in the school yard!) we had a long chat with Zoë's teacher, who had spent some time teaching in the UK.

She said the main difference is that 'kids are allowed to be kids' here and she came up with a very interesting example. In the UK our children play in the school yard but they aren't allowed skipping ropes, sports equipment, etc. So end up running and pushing each other around. This can obviously lead to fighting and bullying. The lunch break at Zoë's school however sees the children using all types of sporting equipment – basketball, hockey, football – and they can even take a swim in the outdoor pool.

In the short time we have been here we have been invited to all sorts of shows and dances that the children have done and the parents are very much involved in school life. They have to be as money is in short supply with a smaller population and so parents help out on trips and even at lunch breaks.

We had heard all sorts of opinions on New Zealand education before our move but I can honestly say that Zoë loves going to school here and we feel that a whole range of opportunities will open up for her the further she goes. The main thing we feel she will get from her education here that she may have missed in the UK is the sense of independence Kiwi kids seem to have from being allowed to explore things for themselves.

## MONEY WORRIES

So Zoë and Sam were settling in well and making new friends while Julie and I were beginning to wonder if we were getting ourselves into a situation we couldn't get out of. We worked out the cost of living here on a weekly basis and compared it with the amount I was earning. The simple fact was that we could not expect to live off a brand new business that needed time to grow.

The house in the UK needed to be sold or we would run out of money very quickly. The next few months were definitely the scariest time of my life. Since the children were born I had always worked and, although we had struggled, luckily I had never had to worry about putting food on the table.

On days when I had no bookings I would set off in the van with a handful of flyers and cold call on all the local businesses. Sometimes I would do this for days with very little or no interest being shown. Julie would phone to see how I was getting on and I wished I could give her some good news. In fact, if somebody had said they thought our business was a really good idea (a lot did) I would tell Julie, only for her to ask, 'Why didn't they book us then?'

Each day like this added to the financial pressure and worry and, although we now had an offer in on the house in the UK, we realised it was going to be a long hard slog to get the lifestyle we came here for, even with the money from the UK. We knew the NZ wage is lower than the UK – in fact the average seems to be somewhere around $10 per hour – but it really doesn't hit you until you start to earn it.

Generally the cost of living here is only slighlty lower than in the UK. Food is about the same and house prices are rising, as are council rates, etc. The only thing that is cheaper is motoring costs and insurance, so in reality, even though we had a huge mortgage in the UK, out here we were financially worse off than we had ever been. Julie started to look for work just to get us through but with wages at $10 an hour or less, and by the time we added Sam's nursery fees into the equation she was better off continuing to help me with Car Care. We were arguing a lot at this point, both with each other and with the estate agent in the UK, and so after a another day of driving around looking for work I decided to head for home, feeling completely fed up. In some ways living in a place as beautiful as this makes it worse because it's like walking around paradise with your hands tied. The life we wanted was all around us but it may as well have been a million miles away.

## MY FIRST BREAK

Then my mobile rang – it was a booking to groom 20 Rover cars for a local car yard. This meant I was fully booked for that week and the next and was the first turning point in the growth of the business.

In Tauranga a referral is the best way of getting business in the long term. It means you have regular clients, but in the initial stages of establishing a business it means you are caught in a horrible 'catch 22' situation. People won't book you unless you have been recommended but if you haven't done any work how can anyone recommend you?

I couldn't believe I had come all the way out to New Zealand and was grooming cars made by one of the companies I worked for in the Midlands. Whilst working on these cars I started getting my first referrals from the owners of the car yard and I was soon booked for the next week and the week after that – in fact since that job, work has grown on a steady basis.

I have recently joined the BNI (Business Networking Institute) after seeing the results referrals can achieve. The smaller population in New Zealand is attractive to us in the UK but it has its downside if you want to be establish your own business. If this is an option you are looking at then be prepared for a lot of hard work and frustration, and do look at something like the BNI.

### HOMESICKNESS HITS

So far  I hadn't experienced homesickness, although Julie was suffering badly. Then one night I had a dream about my dad and woke up the next morning with this horrible feeling that this wasn't my home. I guess the only way to describe it is a feeling of terrible isolation and alienation. I felt distant from everything I was doing that day and no matter how hard I tried I couldn't shake the feeling.

We have heard of families from the UK who have come here and given in to homesickness, some after as little as two months, some after as long as three years. Up until that day I couldn't understand why, but it really is something you have to expect and try to get through.

We always said that we would stay here at least until we can get citizenship for the children, which will give them the opportunity to live in NZ, the UK or Australia without going through the process we have had to go through. This is our aim: no matter how hard things get we want to do this for our children.

The strange thing with homesickness is that it will be something you took for granted that sets it off, like remembering somewhere you used to walk the dogs or a regular route that you travelled in the car. Someone asked me the other day if New Zealand felt like home yet and I can honestly say that it doesn't and I have my doubts if it ever will. We hear stories all the time about British people who have gone back to the UK only to feel homesick for New Zealand, and this could end up being a very costly exercise, so when the homesickness arrives just try to get through it.

Missing family and friends is a completely different problem. Time heals but there isn't a day goes by that we don't think about somebody we left behind. You miss the small things such as popping round for a cup of tea or getting advice on a trivial problem you may have.

Luckily, calls to the UK are quite cheap and we can chat for up to two hours for $8. It was during one of these chats with my dad that he put things in perspective by saying how he had only seen my brother, who lives nearby in Derby, once since we left the UK, and when my parents come to visit us early next year for four weeks they will have spent more time with us than with my brother.

Our aim is to be able to visit the UK every other year, with parents visiting us in between or meeting us for joint holidays in the USA. It will mean us earning a lot of money, though, and the reality is most New Zealanders including expats probably only get to visit the UK once you are every five years.

Something else that needs careful consideration when moving here is the fact that once you're here and living on NZ dollars it is very likely that you will lose a lot of money if you move back to the UK – or you may not even be able to afford to make the move! Do your sums and try to have a get-out plan if everything does fail!

## KIWI CULTURE

We slowly began to get used to the Kiwi culture. We still noticed how friendly people were in general but we also began to notice the plain fact that human beings are the same the world over and eveyone has their faults. It was probably a case of losing the rose tinted glasses, but we started to notice things like graffitti and vandalism, although we didn't notice crowds of kids hanging around like they do in the UK.

One thing that was becoming evident was that the New Zealand sense of humour is very different to ours. I can remember the banter that went on between workmates in the factory and it was usually based on insulting each other. Try to do that over here and most Kiwis will take offence and appear to have no sense of humour at all. This isn't true, of course, but the Kiwi sense of humour is definitely more subdued.

Recycling was also something we had to get used to and we had to order two different bins for the house, one for general waste and the other for glass, plastic and paper (to be recycled). The Kiwis like to protect their enviroment and it's good to be a part of that.

## NO WORRIES

The chaotic organisation that Julie mentioned in the school also seems to be a Kiwi trait. We were asked to judge a 'battle of the bands' contest being held in Tauranga after introducing ourselves to the staff at the local music shop.

Eugene who works there had almost single-handedly been trying to kickstart the local music scene for the last few years and was very happy to hear of our musical background. He asked if I would help him compère one of the heats that coming Saturday and I jumped at the chance of meeting local musicians. Then the night before the heat, Eugene phoned to say he had forgotten about a gig he was appearing at and would I run the whole thing? Well, I had done this before and so agreed, although I wasn't quite sure what to expect.

I met Eugene before he had to leave and he said everything was in hand. The place was packed and I didn't know anybody so I was introduced to Karl, the sound engineer, and given a list of bands who were due to appear – so far so good. It was only when I dug a little deeper that I began to panic. Eugene calmly informed me that two of the bands hadn't turned up yet and when I asked about equipment sharing, it turned out one of these bands had an amp the other bands were supposed to be using. No one except me seemed bothered by this and so I decided to relax and take it all in my stride.

The amazing thing was that, despite my not knowing how long each act was allowed on stage or who was in which band, or which band was on next (all things I would have planned to the last detail), the evening ran really smoothly. People just seemed to muck in and help each other. I remember thinking how if this was my gig in the UK I would have been running round like a headless chicken trying to prevent problems that probably weren't going to happen. I have been to nights like this since and the same 'take it in your stride' attitude is always there. There is a popular saying here and I must admit I picked it up very quickly: 'no worries'. It seems like a healthy outlook to me.

## TELEVISION AND RADIO

In these first few months we complained to each other how poor the television shows are here, and the amount of adverts per programme (more than anywhere in the world) was annoying to the point where we actually didn't watch much TV.

UK culture really seems to be based around sitting in front of the TV all night and going to the pub at weekends. The pub culture here is replaced with a café culture and the TV really isn't good enough to watch all night. We were, however, starting to get into some of the American series that dominate schedules her, and some of the adverts were the funniest and most shocking we have ever seen.

The use of, shall we say, 'colourful' language also jumps out at you. I remember watching breakfast TV one morning and looking up as the interviewer came out with the dead pan statement, 'That's bollocks!' Certain words here aren't even classed as swearing and the first time I heard a morning radio presenter say, 'Now phone in to play the bastard of a teaser and you could win a fridge full of piss' (beer) I nearly spat my cornflakes across the room.

## MACHO MEN

There is a definite macho sort of culture among men here that is evident in fast cars, sport, drinking and putting down the fairer sex. One taxi driver, who was struggling to fold Sam's pushchair, asked Julie how it was done and once she had shown him he proceeded to joke how he knew nothing about pushchairs but could operate a clutch and did Julie know where the clutch was on the car? It's something to be aware of but again is a generalisation.

Some people told us New Zealand was like the UK but with better weather. The culture really does take some getting used to though. I bumped into a Brit who had moved out here four weeks earlier and he said he had never felt so 'alien'.

I know I haven't mentioned Maori culture but that is because I really haven't had much time to look into it. It is something that interests me and I am sure that on our travels around the country I will have a chance to encounter it. After all, New Zealand is one of the newest countries in the world and the Maori culture plays a large part in life here.

All in all, the people we meet are still generally more friendly and relaxed than in the UK with a subtle sense of humour and independent outlook on life. People do enjoy outdoor activities, and socialising at night is more family orientated, with children being allowed in most bars or restaurants. As in all societies, however, there is an unruly element, lovingly referred to as 'hoons'.

## DANGER ON THE ROADS

'Hoons' are bored teenagers generally and their favourite pastime is cruising around in fast cars with huge exhaust and music systems. This is fine by me but it does get out of hand when they race or drive wrecklessly. New Zealanders can drive a car at 15 years old, and add to that the fact that they don't need to insure the vehicle and you have a recipe for disaster. So you have a lot of youngsters driving around in fast cars trying to impress their mates. There is also a high proportion of drunk drivers added into the mix, due to the fact that taxis are expensive and public transport is virtually non-existent except in the major cities. The number of deaths on New Zealand roads is shocking and we seem to read of a fatality in the local paper most weeks.

So when you do come here, even for a holiday, always be alert on the road and beware the left-hand rule. This involves stopping when turning into a road on the left (even though it is clear) to allow someone who is turning right into the same road to do so first. Confused? You will be!

*Previous page:* The Goddards on Moturiki Island, off Mount ◀ Maunganui beach.

Paul with his Car Care van. ▲

The Goddard family home in Tauranga. ▶

Sail Away concert, Tuapiro Point, Upper Tauranga harbour. ◀

Boats, Tauranga
Rail Bridge. ▲

View from ▶
Plummers Point
towards the end of
Te Puna Peninsula.

Sailing in Tauranga
harbour, with
Mount Maunganui
behind. ◀

Statue of Wairaka ▲
on rock at the
Whakatane River.

Tauranga Harbour
Bridge, near where
the Goddards live.
◄

Surf on rocks and ▶
gnarled
pohutakawas,
Mauao base track.

Autumn trees,
McLarens Falls
Park. ▲

View from Whakapapa
skifield, Mount Ruapehu,
North Island. ▼

Café culture in mall,
Tauranga          ▶

Mount Hytt, Rakaia
Gorge. ▲

Waikato River,
Hamilton, North
Island. ▶

Whaitangi, Bay
of Islands, North
Island. ◀

Southern Alps, South Island. ◄

Rural Wanaka, ► golden fields lying between the huge mountain range of the Southern Alps.

The poplar trees of Roy's Bay, Lake Wanaka, South Island. ▼

Rippon vineyard, ▲
central Otago,
South Island.

Onslow, Otago, ▶
South Island.

*Following page:*
Pohutukawa trees.

The Church of the
Good Shepherd,
Lake Tepako in
Mackenzie County,
South Island. ◀

## CRIME LEVELS IN THE NEIGHBOURHOOD

We were invited to a neighbourhood watch meeting shortly after moving into the new house and so went along, hoping the news about local burglary figures wouldn't be too shocking as all our belongings were due to arrive from the UK soon. It was a good turn out and a nice way to meet the neighbours, and after coffee and biscuits we got down to the dreaded statistics.

There had been four burglaries and a 'hoon' had damaged someone's tree. This wasn't good – four burglaries in one week in such a small area seemed a lot. Then the penny dropped: we were talking about the total number of burglaries since the group was formed a few months earlier. We were further informed that most of these could have been prevented if people had closed their windows when leaving the house!

Most of the homes near us don't have alarm systems, although this trend is slowly changing. There are all sorts of crimes committed here, but the main difference seems to be that it is on a much smaller scale, and with the smaller population the best deterrent is the fact that you are more likely to be caught. We left the neighbourhood watch meeting quite happy, but decided to find out how much an alarm system would cost (around $500).

Our parents were sending us copies of the local newspaper from home, as we were getting publicity prior to the BBC series going on air. We sat comparing news stories from both towns. It really was an eye-opener and reminded us of some of the reasons we left the UK.

## OUR BELONGINGS ARRIVE

The new house was feeling more like home now but still seemed very bare. Then the phone rang. It was the delivery people saying our container had arrived and could they deliver it this Friday. I put the phone down and it was all systems go. We decided to paint the children's bedrooms in the style they had at the old house to help them feel more settled.

We had actually brought the wall decorations for Sam's room that he had in the UK out with us. Even though we were renting so couldn't make alterations until the house was ours, we went hunting for paint. Now paint in New Zealand is very expensive compared to the UK, but luckily it spreads well and I managed to paint both rooms in two nights just in time for the 96 packages to be dropped off on the Friday morning.

The boxes were unloaded from the van into the various rooms with Julie supervising the whole thing. Then it really was like a long Christmas day opening presents. The kids were really excited as all their toys were here; some were even unopened from Christmas as we had left in such a hurry.

Now you've probably gathered that when it comes to getting things done we don't hang around, so over the weekend both the children's rooms were decorated, everything was unpacked and re-built and even pictures were hung on the walls. I think the guys from the removal company were a little shocked when we phoned on the Monday asking them to pick the empty boxes up!

This weekend of activity took our mind off everything and if felt like we were finally starting to build a home.

The weather was still really hot and I was losing a lot of weight as I was working in the sun. I only noticed when I tried on some of my clothes which had just arrived. Sam loved his room and he really did seem to settle easier with his familiar stuff around him. I ventured into the attic for the first time because, although we had a massive clearout before we left for NZ, there are always those sentimental things you keep in the attic gathering dust. I couldn't believe the size of the space up there – maybe in the future we will make it into a room.

Out of 96 boxes we had no breakages or missing items, so a big thumbs up to John Masons. We have heard nightmare stories from people who have paid twice the fees we did to ship their belongings only to find much of it broken or missing. One family even told us they could see where the boxes had been cut open and valuables removed.

Try to use a company that has been recommended to you. The British expats website is a great resource for this sort of thing (www.britishxpats.com). The only thing we needed now to complete the family were our two Cavalier King Charles spaniels. They were due to arrive in two days' time via Sydney. Julie was worried about how they would cope on the flight, but again, Golden Arrow shippers had been recommended to us and when we left them we were very impressed with the set up.

Shipping dogs to New Zealand isn't difficult, but it is costly. We paid the going rate of around £2000 to ship our two out, but Golden Arrow were very helpful and explained exactly what we needed to do – basically taking them to the vet for jabs and for microchips to be inserted. They even let the dogs stay with them for five weeks prior to shipping which helped us as we had enough to do with all the packing, without the dogs getting under our feet.

There is no quarantine when bringing dogs from the UK so we drove up to Auckland airport to pick them up. There was a quick form to sign at the Customs office and we were taken to where the dogs were being kept. They were still in their purpose built boxes and although a bit subdued seemed to be fit and well. We walked them to a designated 'toilet area' and stood for what seemed like ages as the dogs did their 'business'.

So that was it – we were now a complete family and the only remaining link to break with the UK was our house. Little did we know how much grief that was going to give us over the coming months.

## SHALL WE STAY OR SHALL WE GO?

As we settled into our new life we were beginning to realise a few things. There were lots of little costs that we hadn't considered in our plans because we didn't think they would be big enough to matter. However, with the Kiwi dollar all money matters and small payments for contents or health insurance all started to add up. Our funds were diminishing rapidly and then the bill arrived that was finally going to force us to sell up and go back to the UK.

The van I bought for the business was being paid off in installments because we hadn't sold the house and so I wanted to keep as much money as possible for a 'cushion' while the business was growing. However, with the house still not sold, those funds were nearly gone. On top of that, I had a one-off payment which I had agreed to – thinking the house would be sold by the time it was due – and this was going to wipe us out. In addition the mortgage repayments in England were about to restart and we were struggling to pay the rent here. Selling up seemed to be the only option.

This was the worst time of our lives so far. To be forced to sell up and return just a few months into our new life simply because our house in the UK hadn't sold just wasn't fair. In the weeks leading up to this point we had been frantic trying to think of ways we could get out of this situation. We don't come from rich families and so we could get no help there and the banks here wouldn't help us as we had no equity. It was so frustrating: we had left the UK with an excellent credit rating and I couldn't even get a temporary overdraft facility on my business account here.

Julie and I were really under pressure and when Julie's homesickness was added to the equation it sometimes felt that going back to the UK would be the easier option. We couldn't sleep at night and the days were miserable.

We also had people who had seen video tapes of the programme featuring us stopping us in the street and telling us to stick it out. At the time it was the last thing we needed as we knew that once the direct debit came out for the van we were broke. It had been a long time since I'd had to wonder where we were going to get money for food but this was now the reality.

## DESPERATE MEASURES

I decided to speak to Lorraine from Car Care about our situation and she offered to come and visit us. It was a very emotional meeting for all of us as none of us wanted this to be happening. We discussed selling the business and looked at all the options. In the end help came from two directions. As Lorraine wanted us to suceed as much as we did, she put up the money for the van payment and I agreed to pay it back as soon as the house in the UK had sold.

We also phoned the bank manager in Coventry, who had been great with us in the past. He suggested reducing the mortgage payments to interest only and offered us a £2500 overdraft facility on our account in the UK, even though there was no money going into it. Obviously the bank was covered because they would get the money from the house, but it was great of them to do this for us and it meant we had a few more months to sell the house. We had been given a bit of breathing space but this definitely wasn't why we had moved to New Zealand.

Three months in and we were financially worse off than we had ever been. Even though I was trying to remain positive, I knew we could easily end up being in the same situation two months from now. We set ourselves a deadline of one month for things to turn around. There was an offer in on the house that we had accepted, but we were in a chain and we didn't hold out much hope. The only way out was to boost business somehow. I decided to take the van down to golf clubs on weekends to try and tempt people into getting their cars groomed while they played golf.

On the first visit I was really busy and people were commenting on what a great idea it was. However, as with most of the good ideas I had tried so far, interest soon dwindled. The business was growing at a natural pace and probably slightly ahead of what we had planned, but we still needed a boost. Things were just getting more and more frustrating. We had ideas but we didn't have the capital.

## I WANT TO GO HOME

Julie really wanted to call it quits and go home, and I couldn't think of an immediate solution to our problems. The children definitely didn't want to go home. Zoë was loving school and we could see Sam was happy, although he was probably picking up on the atmosphere around the house and started saying that he was missing home and wanted to see Grandma and Nanna and Grandad.

It really is horrible when you are in a situation like this with no family to back you up. We couldn't give the children pocket money and our three-year-old boy was saying he wanted to go home. I just kept saying to Julie, 'we'll get through this' and I honestly believed that in the long term there would be more opportunies for us here than in the UK.

With New Zealand being such a new country a lot of things we take for granted – like the rehearsal studio – just haven't been tried here. Tauranga has a massive proportion of self-employed people and you constantly bump into entrepenuers looking for the next big idea. It makes things difficult and competitive but there is a general sense that you can make it and there are a lot of people around here who have done just that.

## A SLIGHT IMPROVEMENT

I know a lot of people would have given up at this point, but we dug in and kept pushing the business. It slowly turned around and after a while I didn't have to sit around on golf course car parks at weekends – I still clean my car and van at the local shopping plaza every Sunday, though. We were nearly making enough money to cover the bills each week and weren't dipping into our own funds as much. The problem hadn't gone away, but we were just waitng for the call to say contracts had been signed on the house. I do think if we hadn't had children though I would have called it a day at this point, but their future was such a big motivation for us being here that I wasn't going to give up.

# Chapter Three

# Getting Settled

**Finally we had the phone call we had waited eight months for: contracts for the sale of our house had been signed! The strange thing was that althought his was a big relief and meant we didn't have to sell up and move back, we didn't get excited about the sale. I guess deep down we still knew life would be a bit of a struggle here for a while yet. Although a lot of Brits have moved out here after making a fortune on their houses we weren't one of those lucky few and would still have a fairly big mortgage here. It did, however, mean we could finally look at a future here in New Zealand and was the boost we needed to make things happen for us.**

For the last few weeks I had started going to a bar called 'Krazy Jack's' on a Wednesday night. Eugene – the guy I mentioned earlier from the music shop – had started an acoustic night when anyone could get up and have a go. He introduced me to a guy called Derrin who is a local guitar tutor. It turned out we had the same taste in music and so we decided to do a few covers with a view to earning some money at the weekends. It felt great to be singing on stage again, and although I was more nervous than I could ever remember being, my confidence as a singer was returning.

Krazy Jack's is a great little bar right on the harbour front and a lot of local musicians go there, so Eugene began introducing me to everyone and told them about the rehearsal rooms we had in Coventry. It soon became obvious that the local bands were really struggling to find somewhere to rehearse and so I had a chat with Julie about setting up a rehearsal studio with some of the money from the house sale.

## A NEW BUSINESS IDEA

The way I saw it was that we had two major problems with our new life so far. First was the fact that we were missing all our friends and second we were under a lot of financial pressure with setting up a new business. The rehearsal rooms could help by enabling us to meet like-minded people and give us a second income. We could live off Car Care eventually, but with so much to do we wanted to have the financial stability we were used to.

The only downside, apart from the risk factor, was the fact we could end up working the long hours we had come to New Zealand to get away from. So we did a little research and put together a business plan.

With most young Kiwis earning around $10 per hour we figured we could employ someone to help run the rooms. Karl, who we had met at the 'battle of the bands' had already told us he would love to help out. We phoned him up for a chat and it turned out Karl had a load of local contacts and some great ideas.

This was looking more and more like a good idea but we were a lot more wary after seeing how long it had taken our other business to get going. We would be throwing a big chunk of our savings into this second business and so we would need it to work almost immediately.

Then came our first set back! I phoned NZ immigration to explain what we wanted to do and they wouldn't allow it. We would have to give up Car Care and apply for a new long-term business visa for the rehearsal studio. This seemed crazy to me as Car Care was growing and we could run both businesses by employing somebody.

Not being people to sit back and take things we decided to write to the Prime Minister, as we had met her, and she is also Minister for the Arts. This was a hell of a long shot, but we received a letter one week later from her office saying she had forwarded the matter to the immigration minister. We couldn't even believe we had got a reply, let alone so quickly!

The business plan was done and we continued our plans, even though we could be turned down by the immigration minister. Then just days after the first letter, a letter arrived from the immigration minister's office saying that there was nothing to stop us setting up the rehearsal studio and all we had to do was let Immigration know what we were doing.

This was fantastic news and the next step was to look for premises. I had joined the BNI (Business Networking Institute) to grow our business and used my contacts with local estate agents there to find us suitable premises. However, the fact that it had to be fairly big and in a non-residential area meant this was going to be a hard task. We looked at a few premises but none were suitable. The agents said that was all there was, and after driving around ourselves we began to believe them. All we could do was sit and wait for something to turn up and in the meantime concentrate on Car Care.

Things were still financially tight, so now we had contracts in place for our house sale I decided to ask the bank for an overdraft facility until the money arrived, or a credit card. I even took in the email from the estate agents in the UK saying the contracts were completed. The bank said they were sorry but as we still didn't own the property here they couldn't help us.

I have said before that recommendations in business are a good thing – well, ASB bank was recommended to us and although the service had been good we felt they could have done a little better. After all, we had a business account with them, an excellent credit history in the UK (which means nothing out here) and a pre-approval for a mortgage.

I was moaning to one of my regulars about our situation and he said that National Bank would be able to help and gave us the manager's number. National Bank told us they would give us mortgage approval, a credit card and an overdraft facility on the business account. ASB lost our custom the next day. To me all banks are more or less the same, but it's the ones that will go the extra mile that attract your loyalty.

On the subject of commerce, I have noticed that in terms of banking New Zealand is on a par with the UK; in fact, with the EFTPOS system they may be slightly ahead. This is as close to a cashless society as we have ever seen. The bank issues you with an EFTPOS card – much like a cashpoint card – and you choose your own four-digit PIN number.

The difference is that virtually every business has an EFTPOS facility (including me). So if you go to a bar for a drink you just swipe your EFTPOS card through the reader, enter your PIN and $3.00 is instantly deducted from your bank account. The fact that everyone accepts EFTPOS means we very rarely carry cash around.

## TV CELEBRITIES

It was beginning to look like there was a light at the end of the tunnel, albeit a small one. The house was sold but we still had to wait for the money. We had permission to set up a new business but were struggling to find premises.

The *Get a New Life* TV programme had just been aired in the UK and was having a positive effect. We started getting recognised in the street by people who had relatives in the UK who had sent video tapes over. We used the opportunity to promote the business and had articles in the local press about our move. We even had a booking via a guy in Sweden who phoned his father in Tauranga after seeing the show to say that he should book his car in for a groom. We were being recognised at least twice weekly and the show hasn't even been on TV here.

When we were first asked to get involved with the programme we weren't sure, as we knew it would be a stressfull enough time without having TV cameras around, but it turned out to be a very enjoyable time and certainly opened a few doors for us. Most of the people who recognised us were obviously Brits and a few were in a similar position to us, having just moved here. Some were even just visiting to check the country out and wanted our advice on emigrating. As Car Care is a franchise it was very easy for people to get hold of us and as well as all the emails, we started getting phone calls from the UK.

Unfortunately we didn't have much in common with most of the people who came up to us as they tended to be a lot older.

Then one day Julie was stopped by a girl called Beth while shopping in Tauranga. It turned out Beth and her husband Tom had moved to New Zealand about ten months previously and had recently relocated to Tauranga. The crazy thing was they were originally from Nuneaton, which was just a few miles down the road from us in Coventry. They were our age and were going through the same experiences, so a friendship formed and we are still in touch regularly.

Another guy got in touch with me via email and said he was coming to check the place out and could he meet with us. Gavin was from Plymouth and again we got on well (he had already emigrated to America so knew what to expect) and he helped Julie get through her first bout of serious homesickness by telling us of his experience in the USA. We keep in touch and he is moving out here with his family later this year. We wouldn't have met these people if we hadn't been in the show but I must admit I think we will go into hiding for a few weeks if it ever does get shown over here!

Brighter Pictures, who made the show, were also keeping in touch via email to see what we were up to. Then one day they asked if we would agree to being filmed for an update. So it looked like we were going to be on TV again. The timing was perfect as the date they said they were arriving was the day after our money was due to be released from the house sale. The local estate agent also phoned that week to say he had found a unit that might be suitable.

## A NEW CAR

We decided to celebrate by trading in the car we had bought for something a little sportier. Cars in New Zealand come in all shapes and sizes and you do notice a lot of older models on the roads. The majority are imported from Japan and sell at a much lower price than in the UK . Insurance here is also a lot cheaper in comparison so we decided to buy a Subaru Impreza WRX. There was no way I could have afforded to run or insure a car like that in the UK, and this was one of the reasons we had moved here – to be able to do things we couldn't at home.

So we bought the car from Tony Hammond, a car dealer here in Tauranga who had helped us out when we first arrived by giving me some work. I phoned the insurance company from his office and they said the car was a high risk vehicle so they would have to get some advice. I sat there waiting, thinking that we had just signed to buy this car and now we were going to be stung by high insurance payments.

The girl came back on the phone and was sorry to tell us that because the car was a high risk the insurance would be $360 per year! That's only £110! Welcome to motoring NZ style. Petrol is cheap and diesel cheaper still, but you do pay a levy for using a diesel vehicle. Although New Zealand actually produces more methane from its livestock than fumes from cars, which has led to a proposed 'fart tax' for farmers (no, I'm not joking).

Another great thing here is that for $500 you can buy a personalised number plate. It can be any combination of letters or numbers up to six digits. So as long as nobody has already chosen your plate you can come up with gems such as 'surfin' or 'ngoti8', which is on one of the local estate agent's vehicles. This doesn't have the snob factor that comes with a personalised plate in the UK. In fact Kiwi's really don't seem to care for that whole 'keeping up with the Joneses' attitude. If you go to the shops in the evening you will regularly see kids shopping with their parents in their slippers and nightclothes. Some people might see this as laziness but why bother getting dressed to go to the shops only to put your nightclothes back on as soon as you are back home? Mind you, I haven't quite taken to going out in my slippers yet and my bare feet look pretty disgusting too!

It was looking like the BBC would have plenty to film while they were here and I received a booking for my biggest job yet, grooming six brand new Subaru Foresters for a press launch at a lodge in Rotorua. This was the first time any franchisee for Car Care NZ had been asked to groom for a press launch, so I would have to make sure I did well, especially with the camera's on us. I used to prepare cars for press launches as part of my job in the UK so I was confident I could pull it off. I also knew that the car companies usually choose a stunning location so it would be great footage for the TV programme.

Car Care was in another upswing when the crew arrived and I was actually fully booked for the whole week. We had sorted out with the estate agent to look at some premises for the rehearsal studio and I was going to be singing at Krazy Jack's on the Wednesday night. One of my friends from the BNI had arranged a flight in a glider and another friend at the BNI had invited us to spend a day at their adventure park. We met the crew and explained what we had going on and they looked quite worried as they would only be spending a week with us.

We soon settled in to being filmed again. We decided to push the business by contacting the local press for interviews and I was asked to appear on the local radio station as well. We have always jumped at opportunities and taken risks as I truly believe you make your own luck. It's not everyday you get asked to appear in a TV programme so we needed to push the business as much as possible and it's a great way of getting known. I think if the program gets shown over here I'll probably need to employ someone to help me with all the extra orders I'll get for Car Care.

Things were a little more laid back with the filming this time as we were more settled. We were asked a lot of questions on camera and had to do a little soul searching, which could be quite hard, especially when talking about family and friends in the UK. It was good finally to show people our new life and see what they thought of it. They caught us at a very positve time as the money from the house sale had finally come through and we were trying to set up the rehearsal studio.

## SETTLING IN

The week the BBC arrived to film the update was a turning point for our fortunes. It's funny, but no matter how bad things get, life goes on and finds its own way of sorting things out. We had almost run out of money and then the house finally sold. We wanted extra income to enjoy the lifestyle here and we had been given permission to set up the rehearsal studio.

We didn't know how long this change in fortune would last but decided to make the most of it. The first thing on the agenda was the job at Rotorua. We drove down early in the morning as it takes around 45 minutes to reach Rotorua from Tauranga and grooming six cars would take most of the day.

Rotorua is one of the most popular tourist destinations in New Zealand, mainly due to all the volcanic activity in the region. It also has some of the best fishing in the world and the scenery can be breathtaking – as can the sulphuric smell, which is ever present. We had visited the town on our fact-finding trip back in October and unfortunately hadn't been very impressed. However, subsequent visits through work had changed my perspective on the place and I now discover something new every time I am down there.

The lodge was in a beautiful setting on the edge of the lake and even though it was winter (I had to wipe ice off the cars) the sun was shining. I can remember thinking that when the footage from this job gets shown people will think it was a set up for the program but I do actually get asked to do work in locations like this quite often – this is New Zealand, after all.

One of the great things about the business we bought is that Julie and I can work together and quite often we will bring the kids along. On a job like this the kids go and play on the sandy lakeshore while we work, which is great and is part of the family life we were missing out on in the UK. Even when I am working in Tauranga I will arrange to meet Julie and Sam for lunch whenever possible. The job went well and the Subaru people were happy, so we headed off back home.

## LOOKING FOR A REHEARSAL STUDIO

The next day we had arranged to meet the estate agent to look at a unit he felt might be suitable as a rehearsal studio. We pulled up at the location, which is near Tauranga's harbour bridge and not ideal as there can be a lot of traffic around. But from the outside the unit seemed large and the rental figure he had mentioned over the phone was very good.

Upon entering we noticed the building was even bigger than we thought, with only half of it viewable from the outside. It had two levels and my brain soon started imagining what it could look like. It was obviously going to take a bit of work to convert and soundproof and the location wasn't ideal, but we left happy that we might be able to make a go of it. The agent told us what a struggle it had been to find a unit even remotely suitable so we decided to make plans.

## WRITING A BUSINESS PLAN

As part of the long-term business visa (LTBV) you have to provide a business plan. This must be one of the questions I have been asked most about the LTBV, 'How do you make your business plan?'. One of the reasons I bought a franchise was that I knew they would have all the facts and figures I needed for my plan as they are an established business idea.

You need to outline the business idea, show predictions of profit and growth and basically try to prove on paper that the business will work. It needn't be complicated; in fact, the simpler the better as long as you put enough details in to show that the business can work. You have to show evidence of research as well, but if you are thinking of setting up a business without doing any research then you are probably doomed to failure anyway.

I would also strongly recommend using a migration agency if applying under the LTBV category, but make sure they have experience dealing with this visa. Apparently virtually anyone can declare themselves a migration agent as there is no required training, so be very careful when choosing one. We have heard nightmare stories of people spending thousands of pounds only to be rejected by Immigration at the end of the process. We paid our agent (the Emigration Group) £800 to check our application and it was money well spent.

We arranged to get a builder round to look at the unit the following week to estimate the cost of soundproofing and building the rooms we needed. Bay Music had sorted out prices of equipment for us and we figured we would be looking at around $20,000 to set up the new business. This doesn't sound a lot when you convert it to UK pounds (around £8,000) but we know people out here who only earn $15,000 per annum. It would actually be half of the cushion of money we had kept back from the sale of the house.

We did this by having part of our mortgage here on what they call 'revolving credit'. This means we chose to put $40,000 of our mortgage onto our normal current account as an overdraft (at mortgage interest rates). We can pay off as much or as little of this overdraft as we want and if in the future we have paid say $20,000 off and decide we need to purchase something then we can go up to the $40,000 limit again without having to apply to the bank for a loan. You have to be disciplined to run this sort of mortgage but it has its advantages if your income can fluctuate as ours does.

## TAURANGA FROM THE AIR

Next on the agenda was my flight in a glider. John Roberts, who I met at BNI, is a trainer at the gliding club here in Tauranga and offered to take me up for a test flight. I wasn't nervous but as I pulled the cord to release the glider from the tow plane and we put the glider into a diving turn my stomach dropped.

The views were amazing as we were flying around Mount Maunganui and along the coast. It was so peaceful but the turbulence really was making me feel ill. The cost of a flight like this is $80 and the cost of learning to become a glider pilot is also relatively inexpensive at around $6000. If you are inclined to become a comercial pilot or professional diver then New Zealand is the place to do it, especially if you have a few spare UK pounds.

Here's a job idea for you: why not train to be a helicopter pilot then get a job or set up a business flying tourists around the NZ scenery? I had that thought one day while driving around looking for work. There really are endless opportunities here if you are prepared to open your mind and take the chances.

John put the glider into one last steep turn and the G force really was quite amazing – my stomach certainly felt it. He set the glider gently down and I staggered out, thrilled but feeling very queasy. I know I could have gone gliding in the UK, or surfing for that matter, but over here it really is made available for everyone and not just the select few with money to burn. As I walked over to Julie and the kids I think she was quite relieved that it wasn't her up in the glider as I did look rather ill.

The next day we took the kids to Waimarino Adventure Park, which is located on the banks of the Wairo River and is owned by Barry and Barbara, who I met at the BNI. Barry bought the place as a swamp 30 years ago and slowly turned it into the adventure park. They have people coming from all over to try their hand at kayaking, climbing and swimming and win awards for local tourism.

We had a great time and the kids especially enjoyed the place. As it was the middle of winter I declined the chance to fly off a water slide in a canoe into the river, although we did go for a swim in the hot pool. Like many places in New Zealand, Waimarino is really geared up for families.

## STARTING TO LIVE THE DREAM

It was nice to think that now the business was giving us a regular income it hopefully wouldn't be long before we could start to take up some hobbies and try out the lifestyle we were aiming for. I guess in hindsight we did what a lot of people looking at coming to New Zealand from the UK do.

The price of things here converted back to pounds gives the impression that the cost of living is really low. I would surf the internet pricing cars, jet skis and boats and convert the NZ dollar to pounds, which fuels the dream as these things suddenly become affordable. The reality is that it will probably take a lot longer than you planned before you can make the dream a reality.

One reality was that we had traded our three-bedroom house in the UK for a four-bedroom dream home in Tauranga and we were now enjoying making it our own. Julie ordered some wooden blinds as the sun can really heat up the house in the summer months, and she used her artistic flair to put our mark on the place. She even put a Union Jack flag with BUSH (her favourite band) written on it, on the wall in the hallway.

The garden is a lot bigger than we were used to, so as the weather was improving we decided to rip up all the rose bushes the previous owners had planted. We thought about putting in a swimming pool but obviously couldn't afford that expense yet – and we have been warned that pools can actually take value off a house because of the high maintainance factor. Why have a pool when the Pacific Ocean is only a ten minute walk away?

So in the end we decided to just grass over the old rosebed. You really can grow anything here so we have planted lemon, orange, grapefruit, passionfruit and lime trees, along with potatoes and tomatoes. All you need to do then is walk to the beach, catch a fish, throw it on the barbeque and you are virtually eating for free. This is actually very popular around here, especially in the summer, and the neighbours will often pop round with their 'catch of the day' for you.

We were also starting to make friends around this time; it had taken us longer than we thought. I guess the fact we couldn't go out much socially didn't help and also the fact that we are constantly moving around working at different locations means we don't actually have any workmates. Friends are what you miss when you emigrate and I must admit it is the hardest part for me.

We figured that setting up a rehearsal studio here would provide us with the opportunity to meet like-minded people, so hopefully in a few months time we will start to get a strong circle of friends. It's funny but I miss being invited to weddings (although I was never actually that bothered about going to them) and the big family get togethers that happen once in a while. Birthdays are hard and Christmas will be very strange, although Julie's mum will be out here with us.

As a family we were definitely becoming closer. Our new regular Sunday afternoon strolls up the Mount or visits to the Papamoa flea market every other weekend have brought us closer. I guess because we are here alone it is sink or swim as far as family relationships go. We have to rely on each other for support and motivation and we are all experiencing new things together.

There can be massive strains, especially when disagreements arise over whether we should have even come here at all. If you move out here you will ask yourself that question many times. Why did we come here? The answer can be more elusive as time goes on.

We are lucky in a way as we have the video of the *Get a new life* programme to remind us. You just have to try to remember the reasons, because it shouldn't be a decision you make lightly and going back without giving it everything you've got really is a waste of time and money.

We were noticing a change in the children as well now. I guess they were enjoying this new family time together, plus the extra freedom they were now experiencing. Zoë had started to invite friends from school to stay and so most weekends we had someone here or Zoë would be at a sleep-over. The extra space in the house means we can have two or three of Zoë's friends round and not really notice they are here. She took to using the phone a lot in the evenings as local calls are free, but this probably has more to do with her age than living in New Zealand!

Sam was enjoying whizzing around the garden on his bike as the weather was improving, and the dogs probably think they've died and gone to heaven! The children were now picking up the Kiwi accent, although Sam's has an American slant to it as he is addicted to watching Nickelodeon on Sky TV. Even I had started to say 'No worries' and 'sweet' and some people were no longer instantly recognising our english accents.

But we still have a long way to go before this feels like home.

## ANOTHER NEW START

We were still debating whether to set up the rehearsal studio – after all, one of the reasons we had come here was to get away from the long hours that this had committed us to in the UK. We had a meeting with a builder who was going to give us a price on the necessary conversion required at the unit we had looked at.

Julie had become even more unsure about the location of the unit and her fears were compounded by our conversation with the builder. Tauranga has a traffic problem in rush hour over the harbour bridge which is right next to the unit. The council has plans to widen the bridge from two lanes to four and the builder told us this work is due to start shortly directly outside the unit. So we had a lucky escape, as we could have taken on this unit only to inherit the problem at a later date.

The film crew left the following morning and as they had only been with us for a week, it wasn't the emotional wrench we experienced after making the first programme. They had asked us some soul searching questions, though, which we would keep in mind over the coming months.

Julie was relieved we hadn't taken the unit on but I really did think that was the end of our plan for a rehearsal studio, as we had looked everywhere for a suitable property. It was then that the builder (sorry I can't remember his name) recommended a friend of his called Jason who builds units to people's specification. Obviously this would be a perfect solution to our problem, so I gave Jason a call. He said he had a unit already built that may be suitable and we could take a look at it.

We drove round and found the unit was on an industrial park with houses quite far away on top of a hill. Jason introduced himself and it turned out he is really good friends with all the people at Bay Music. We looked inside and both of us got very excited as the building seemed perfect. The only problem was that there was only one room that we could soundproof and the other two rooms would need to be built from scratch.

Jason turned out to be a really nice guy and was open to any ideas we had, so after a brief chat it was agreed to get a band in to see what the sound levels would be like outside the unit so that we could decide what soundproofing would be required. The unit had a proper office, a kitchen and rest area and was fairly new and clean we even thought there would be some space for me to pull cars in for grooming when it rained. Eugene from Bay Music offered to get his band down the following night.

We entered the unit in the dark (there was no power so we had to use the generator on my van) and we also had a sound engineer down with us to measure the sound levels from the nearest house. As we expected, the noise levels were way too high, but Jason agreed to give it a go and said he would build the sound proof rooms we required and even put up half the bulding costs. This seemed too good an offer to refuse, so although no contracts had been signed or talked about, it looked like we had finally found some premises.

It would be a lie to say that we had no doubts about setting up this second business and now that we had premises those worries were becoming stronger. This new business would take all of our savings to set up and so would have to at least break even right from the opening week. It could also mean that the free time and lifestyle we had come here for would have to play second fiddle to our workload.

As you might have realised, we are not people to sit down and let life go on around us, so we saw the rooms as a chance to reach our dream lifestyle quicker. We would have to learn from the mistakes we made back in the UK.

The hardest thing about running a successful business is time management and we had fallen into the trap of not organising our time well enough back in the UK. We ran the business between us and in hindsight it was successful enough to employ someone. We started to do a little research and it seemed that apart from the rehearsal side of the business there could be further opportunities here in recording and promotion of the Kiwi bands.

It was obvious we were going to need some help so we decided to ask Karl (who we had met at the battle of the bands) if he would be committed enough to help us out setting the rooms up and eventually work with us. He was more than interested and was a great source of useful contacts. So now there are three of us involved in the rehearsal rooms and hopefully if we are as successful as we were in the UK then we will now also have the time to enjoy that success.

Chapter Four

# Our New Life

**The car valet business was still growing steadily, although the weather was now beginning to affect my income more than ever. We had gone through winter, which was unbelievably short and actually very sunny, and we thought spring would see even drier weather. The opposite happened and it seemed to be raining most mornings. I had bookings but they were phoning up and cancelling because they wanted to wait for the weather to improve. It was frustrating because if these people had booked into a car valet site with premises (i.e. cover from the rain) then they wouldn't have been able to use the weather as an excuse to cancel.**

We were learning a lot more about the reality of being completely self-employed out here than we had done in our previous business and I'm sure it will help us in the long run. I decided to get an accountant as this business was also generating a lot more paperwork than I was used to. I also booked in to get trained on using MYOB (*Mind Your Own Business* software) to enable me to do most of my bookwork via the computer. I would soon be running two businesses and certainly didn't want to run the risk of seeing them go under due to my bookkeeping shortfalls.

Despite the almost constant showers I was now getting advance bookings for the coming week. In addition, the questionnaire we had left at Bay Music, asking bands who may be interested in using a professional rehearsal studio to leave contact details, had returned 16 interested bands. If we could get ten of these bands to rehearse for just two hours per week then we would at least be covering the rent. The building blocks for the businesses were now in place so we decided to take a well-earned break.

## HOLIDAY TIME

We looked at a quick trip to Australia to visit the Gold Coast. It looks great and with the theme parks reminded us of Florida. The airlines seem to be constantly advertising cheap flights across 'the ditch' so we got quite excited about the prospect of a week in Austraila, having heard so much about the place. However, we had limited finances and so the figure of around $3,000 we were being quoted meant that Australia would have to wait.

Our second option was to take a trip to the South Island. We had heard that Christchurch was nice and reminded a lot of people of England so we booked some very inexpensive flights from Rotorura to Christchurch as the drive from Tauranga to Christchurch would have taken a day off the holiday.

Although things have been hard for us here we had managed to see a little of New Zealand on rare weekends off work. Hamilton was one of the first places we had visited and is around an hours drive from Tauranga. It's a big city with plenty to do. The nightlife is excellent and there is a bit of a buzz about the place which was something we were missing from the UK.

There are plenty of parks and the Waikato River runs through the centre of town. The only thing that would put us off living in Hamilton is that the weather doesn't tend to be as good as it is here on the coast. We really enjoy going to Hamilton and I think in some ways it reminds us a litle of the UK. I can't wait to earn enough money so a few of us can go there for a good night out.

We have also spent a day in Whakatane, which is a small coastal town just across the bay from Tauranga. It has some excellent surfing beaches and a very relaxed feel to it. The main attraction is probably White Island, which is New Zealand's most active marine volcano. You can take a boat trip out to the island or fly over in a plane – as long as it's not erupting!

It appears to be a town of contrasts with some old and some very new buildings. Along with most of the towns in the bay, Whakatane is growing quickly as a lifestyle destination. We plan to make trips all over New Zealand but for now (apart from Auckland) that really is all we have seen of the North Island.

## THE SOUTH ISLAND

We had heard and read a lot about the South Island but on the flight down all I could think of was how nice it would be to forget about the financial and business stress we were living with every day. From the air you really do get a sense of how sparsely populated New Zealand is. The scenery was stunning but what struck me was the lack of populated areas.

The country seems completely green, apart from the snow-capped hills and mountains and even cities like Wellington seem small when looking down on them from 25,000 ft. The first thing that strikes you about the geography of the South Island is the mountain ranges. Huge mountains break through the tops of the clouds and it seems a million miles away from the beaches of

Tauranga. The flight takes around two hours and is a great experience for anyone who has never travelled in a propellor driven plane. We touched down at Christchurch airport and although the sun was shining there was a definite drop in temperature.

As we walked from the plane I looked around and was amazed at the stunning scenery. The airfield is surrounded by snowy mountain ranges which stretch as far as the eye can see. I imagined people snowboarding and skiing up on those mountains and was reminded of one of the reasons we came to this beautiful country.

The taxi ride into Christchurch from the airport was a very informative one and the driver even offered to take a free detour through one of the parks, where the flowers are supposed to be quite stunning at this time of year. I must admit I was worried that the description of Christchurch as being New Zealand's most English city would trigger Julie's homesickness again, but as we drove along the main highway we both commented on how it reminded us more of Boston in the USA. The river Avon runs through the centre of Christchurch but it certainly didn't remind us of Stratford, where we had spent many a summer Sunday.

Christchurch is a big city so we had decided to book a one-day tour of the major attractions. This included a gondala ride, the Antarctic Centre, a city tram ride and a visit to the Willow Bank Reserve. The tour was good value but beware when purchasing the tickets in advance. We had to pay addmission for our son Sam on the attractions when if we had purchased the tickets on the gate he would have got in for free due to his age.

The gondala ride provides some great views both of the sea and the mountains in the distance. We had a small snack at the top – don't miss out on the 'time tunnel' as it isn't very clearly signposted but is well worth a look. The Antartic Centre has won awards for being one of New Zealand's best attractions and is very informative. Christchurch is the base for all of the Antartic expeditions and the kids loved the 'snow room'. At Willow Bank, which is a sort of wildlife park, we actually got to see our first live Kiwi birds – although as they are nocturnal, the room was so dark it wasn't a very good view.

We were staying at the Holiday Inn in the centre of town right next to the river Avon. I can thoroughly recommend this hotel, in spite of the pool being extremely cold. The staff were excellent, the food was great and the location is really handy for all the sights. There are plenty of shops in Christchurch and the bus service is a lot better than in Tauranga. You get a sense of history about the place too with the old cathedral and churches; the city planners have done a good job of blending the old with the new. There are lots of excellent cafes and bars too.

I think Christchurch is the first place we visited in New Zealand – apart from Tauranga of course – where we felt we could actually settle. It was turning into just the break we needed and for a few days we forgot about our worries and enjoyed the lifestyle we came here for! The long weekend away went far too quickly and we were soon on the plane heading back to Tauranga.

## WORK AND MORE WORK

Things were starting to get easier for us in some ways now. We had made some friends and the business seemed to be growing, although we still weren't earning enough to live without dipping into our savings. So we had a descision to make: should we forget about setting up the rehearsal rooms and all the pressure that goes with starting a new business and see how much more Car Care could grow, or should we gamble the rest of our money on starting up Backbeat NZ?

We did a lot of agonizing over this question, as the stress of starting Car Care had nearly finished us off, but the reality was that we needed to earn more money or in a year's time we could be facing the reality of having to sell up and go back to the UK. I believe you make your own luck in this life, so we decided to go ahead with Backbeat Rehearsal Rooms NZ.

It was essential that we should keep the set-up costs as low as possible without compromising on quality. We spoke to the agent for Marshall amplifiers and he agreed to sort us out a good price on amps if we stocked exclusively Marshall equipment in the rooms. The price of musical equipment here also seemed to be slightly lower than in the UK, so we worked out a cost of around $16,000 for the equipment we needed. We budgeted on $4,000 for the cost of converting the industrial unit we were looking at, into soundproofed rehearsal rooms.

It was also around this time that Julie suggested we have a go at writing this book, so we were going to be looking at a very busy and stressful time ahead and I was really glad of the break we had just taken. When we had done the sound-level test at the rehearsal rooms, the engineer had said we only needed a reduction of 16 decibels, which we felt could be achieved.

To avoid any potential problem regarding complaints over noise, Jason suggested that we didn't sign any formal contracts regarding the lease of the premises until we were happy that the sound had been reduced enough. This seemed very fair to us and so we started finding out all we could about soundproofing. Our main problem was that the unit wasn't brick built, so sound could easily travel through the steel walls. Jason suggested building an internal room a metre away from the external walls and I suggested we fill the walls of this room and cover the roof with sand.

Three days and $1000 later the room was built and so we started on marketing the business. We rang all the bands on the list we had left at the music shop, but despite great interest found it difficult to pin any of the bands down to actually booking a slot. We would have to come up with some new ideas to make people want to use us.

The good thing about starting from scratch with this business was we could choose the direction we wanted to go in. With Backbeat in Coventry we inherited a lot of the previous owner's choices and had no choice in the layout or room for futher development. Backbeat NZ was going to have to be a little different. We had Karl the sound enginneer on board and plenty of space in the unit, so the logical step would be to install a recording studio. We would also need to set up links with record labels here and in Australia. In other words we would have to offer more than just a rehearsal facility in order to tempt the bands away from their current rehearsal routine.

Car Care was keeping me busy every day now and we certainly couldn't slack off in pushing this business as it was still our only source of income. It did mean that anything to do with Backbeat would have to be done by Julie in the day and me in the evening. Things were starting to get hectic and we found ourselves rushing around again. This was what we came to New Zealand to get away from and both of us were starting to have doubts about what we were doing.

Rick, a drummer from a famous(ish) English band called Blessed Ethel, who I had met through Eugene at Bay Music, offered to help me on the conversion of the rooms and so the four of us (Karl and Julie included) spent the next few evenings laying carpets, cleaning, putting up posters and talking about how good the place was going to be. We were still getting good feedback from people when we explained what we wanted to do with the business, and working in this small team of new friends gave me the camaraderie I had missed since coming out here. With the rooms finished the next step was to get a band in to try it out.

The first NZ band we saw were called Abstract Thought and they kindly volunteered to be the first band to use Backbeat. I was nervous about the noise that would come from the building, despite the considerable amount of soundproofing we had done! Abstract Thought are a very loud band so as they were playing we climbed to the top of the hill behind the studio to see if the noise would annoy the neigbours. It didn't sound too bad and after two hours we hadn't had any complaints.

The band loved the place and said they would spread the word. Backbeat NZ was born, but as with most things we had worked hard to achieve here, Julie and I couldn't get excited as we knew that if we didn't get bands using us we would go under very quickly and may possibly be forced to move back to the UK.

## ROCK 'N' ROLL

A few days after the successful rehearsal we decided to get a music writer from the local press down to the rooms. Winston Watusi writes a well-read column in a local free paper called the *Weekend Sun*. He met us at the rooms and the following Friday wrote a glowing piece all about us and urged bands to use Backbeat. We were excited but despite our optimism we received no phone calls. We had been in contact with the 16 bands who had left contact details for us and had only managed to get one to book in. The stress levels were rising again and I predicted that if things didn't improve we would be looking at selling up and moving back to the UK by spring 2004.

We were frustrated and angry. We had done the reasearch, we had a list of bands who had said they would use us, but once we opened even with the positive press people seemed determined to stay away. I guess it may have had something to do with the relaxed attitude out here but we decided we needed to educate people on what we had to offer.

There was an upcoming  festival called 'Party in the Park' which had 21 bands booked to play. I managed to track down the organiser and offered a prize of a free two-hour rehearsal to one of the bands on the day. There was also an article in the local paper about how the council had identified a real need to make Tauranga attractive to young people. There are a lot of young people here but the town has its 'retirement village' reputation coupled with the fact that a very high per centage of people leave Tauranga between the age of 18 and 25.

We felt Backbeat would help in providing an outlet for the youth of Tauranga and so I got in touch with the councillor who had written the article. Here was another person who agreed the rooms were a great idea but great ideas weren't going to pay the bills. However, she did invite us to the next council meeting and gave me a few contacts who might be able to help promote the business.

One of these contacts was a girl who had set up the Tauranga Youth Trust. It turned out she had received funding to set up a recording studio at one of the local radio stations but the station could no longer accommodate it. This was exciting as here was an opportunity for us to get the recording studio put in almost immediately, so I arranged to meet Rebecca the following Wednesday at Backbeat. Karl joined us at the meeting but Julie had to look after the children, although I promised to let her know what was happening before we committed to anything.

The meeting went well, with Rebecca very interested in putting the studio into Backbeat. A lot of musical projects in New Zealand are funded by various agencies from the government through to churches and this was something I was going to have to learn about if Backbeat was to be a success. A further meeting was scheduled for the following week. Things were looking up, apart from the fact we still only had one band booked in and the phone was very quiet. We also decided to have a sort of open day the following Saturday and the people at the *Weekend Sun* agreed to put another piece in the paper advertising this.

The next few days were horrible. Car Care had been quiet and with no bands booking into Backbeat the stress was beginning to show on Julie and me. For the first time, I seriously considered the option of selling up and going back to the UK. We hadn't signed a contract on the unit for Backbeat so legally we could pull out and we could probably sell Car Care for a profit. We had also made around $50,000 on the house we had bought.

I guess I wanted Backbeat to work and was shocked at the lack of response. I began to weigh up the pros and cons of being in New Zealand and although it was a nice place, the financial stress we had been under from the day we arrived was completely killing my enthusiasm for being here. It came down to one thing – I wasn't going to give up! It's amazing in life that no matter how hard things get, if you keep pushing to achieve your goals eventually something will give. Julie and I had had a few blazing rows over the situation we were in and I did feel like I was failing my family, so when Saturday came around I was praying that some bands would turn up and book slots at the rooms.

The first thing to happen was a couple of phone calls from bands wanting to book in. Then bands started to arrive at the rooms and the feedback we were getting was all good. Students from the local colleges and said they would tell their mates about Backbeat on Monday. A few more bands booked slots for the following week. Although we were a long way from covering the rent, bands had booked in and as we had seen in the UK with

Backbeat, word would spread amongst the musical community. All we needed now was confirmation of the funding for the studio and Backbeat would have the opportunity to grow into something special.

## WORLD FAMOUS IN NEW ZEALAND

Since the TV programme had gone out in the UK we had been stopped in the street here in Tauranga on an almost daily basis. Now we were being recognised even more by Brits either here on holiday or seriously considering relocating to Tauranga. A couple from Manchester stopped us just as we were getting into the car after a relaxing coffee and muffin break – one of our favourite ways to unwind – to say they had just moved here after watching the programme. Not two days later another family stopped us; they had been living in Cyprus, had seen the programme and as they weren't happy there decided to move to Tauranga!

I reckon NZ Immigration should give us permanent residence early for all the people we have indirectly employed here. Making a move like this isn't for everyone and everyone will have different reasons and be in a different situation. When the programme eventually gets shown on TV here I'm hoping business may pick up for a while, but we are not looking forward to telling people that 'yes, Sam's arms are fine now' over and over again.

The amount of emails we receive on a daily basis from the UK is amazing and if anyone reading this has emailed me and I failed to reply, I apologise. We have met Brits out here who are in all types of situations. Some without work, some employed, some like ourselves setting up a business and even some who have been lucky enough to come here and be mortgage free. One thing we all have in common is that even the people without the financial pressure have been tempted to move back to the UK. There are various reasons, for this and an obvious factor is homesickness, but there are a few more common reasons some of which we have experienced and some we have not:

### Missing the buzz

New Zealand has a relaxed lifestyle and that's what attracts people here, but all the people our age (30s) have expressed a strong desire to have a good night out like we used to in the UK. There are nightclubs here and plenty of bars, but definitely not on the scale of the UK.

### Small irritants

A lack of a decent bus service, crazy drivers on the roads, low wages.

### Being miles away

You do feel like a foriegner (yes, I know we are!) but that is a strange feeling to have when you are not used to it. Unless you are lucky it is extremely expensive to get back to the UK and at the moment if we had, for example, a funeral to go to in the UK we would have to get a loan that we can't afford to pay back.

As well as these problems there is simply the adjustment of settling in. After ten months New Zealand doesn't feel like home and I have spoken to expats who have been here for ten years and said that it still doesn't feel like home. These are probably very natural feelings but it is definitely something to be aware of if you do take the plunge.

## FUTURE PLANS

After our meeting with Rebecca from the Tauranga Moana Youth Trust I had to attend a further meeting with the other trust members and the people who were providing the money for the studio. The meeting was very informal; I explained what our vision was for the studio and told them a little about my musical background in the UK. The meeting concluded with an agreement to put the studio into Backbeat and plans to be drawn up as to how we were going to share it between us. This was great news as the recording studio could be another source of income. It was something we had always wanted to have at Backbeat in the UK but we simply lacked the space there.

The Youth Trust was involved with the Party in the Park so it could mean Backbeat growing quicker than we planned or growing in other directions which we haven't envisaged. It could also bring its own complications, but whichever way we look at it the joint venture is a golden opportunity to build a business we have a passion for.

I am tied into Car Care through the business plan that I sent to NZ Immigration for my long-term business visa. However, if Backbeat grows to the point where we need to put all our effort into it then we may have to sell Car Care and start our LTBV from scratch with the new business. At the moment, however, Car Care is paying the bills and Backbeat is running at a loss, so we will have to see how it goes.

We still want to be able to earn enough money to be able to travel back to the UK once in a while, so we could end up in a situation where we have to run both businesses. I guess what I am trying to say is that we have things in place – the two businesses – and we just have to try and make them both work. In our heart of hearts we would love Backbeat to succeed and become our only source of income as it would give us the daytime to enjoy the lifestyle we came here for.

## BUSINESS, MUSIC AND YOUNG PEOPLE IN TAURANGA

With the two businesses to run it was beginning to feel a bit like being back in the UK – although I do still get a good night's sleep here. Setting up the studio made me very homesick and I began comparing NZ bands to UK bands. I also started getting UK music mags like the *NME* and reading these was really making matters worse.

The studio we have here is a better set up than the one we had in Coventry, but the lack of bands coming through the door was very disheartening. I guess we were known around the music scene in Coventry and here we have to earn people's respect by showing them what we can do. It is also a new idea, so the idea of linking up with the local Youth Trust excited me, as they may have contacts that would take us months to find.

Rebecca came to the rooms again for another chat and to go through some legalities of the joint venture regarding the studio. It all seemed pretty straightforward and the Youth Trust seemed to be wanting to get more involved than I previously thought. They mentioned being based at the unit in return for us using their equipment (computers, etc.) and also offered to try and secure further funding or sponsorship.

Julie and I had a chat – Julie has a good head for business when it comes to ideas – and she suggested that we don't rush into sharing the unit with people we hardly know, but wait until the studio is up and running and then decide. After all, we had only just set up the business ourselves and were still getting used to Backbeat being open.

Other parties began showing an interest in the rooms as well, although not bands, but notably the council in Tauranga. I was invited to a meeting as Tauranga council, as mentioned previously, want to make the city more attractive to youth and see it portrayed less as a retirement destination. The meeting focused on ideas for future plans the council may implement regarding its youth policy.

I found there are some serious issues regarding the way the youth of Tauranga are percieved amongst the older generation. Some of these issues came to light through my research into setting up Backbeat, as I was trying to find out as much as I could from young people as to what they want to see happen in the city regarding music. The following story is a good example.

Every New Year's Eve a festival is held in the Mount area of Tauranga and in recent years it has been marred by what the local press describe as 'riots'. One of the bands who had started using Backbeat told us how they were asked to play at last year's festival but received a call a few days before asking if they played distorted guitars. The band said that they did and were subsequently dropped from the festival as it had been decided that this sort of music would cause a riot!

What these people fail to see is that people cause trouble when they are bored or unhappy about something, so if this band had been allowed to play then the kids could have burned off some energy and enjoyed themselves and maybe the riot wouldn't have happened. The youth here seem to be told that they can't do this or can't do that and it is as if the older generation don't want to acknowledge the fact that there are a lot of young people here in Tauranga. The serious side to all of this is that New Zealand has one of the highest teenage suicide rates in the world, so hopefully the council will take some steps to make Tauranga a better place for young people.

I got invited to a follow-up meeting to be held in December and was asked if I would be able to give a ten-minute presentation on Backbeat. Everybody we spoke to said what a great idea the rooms were but we were still not getting enough interest from the bands themselves, even though they too were saying it's a great idea. The fact that music in New Zealand is heavily funded may mean we have to look at the business in a different way to how we did in the UK. There are various aspects to Backbeat NZ that could possibly be eligible for funding or sponsorship and if we could secure this then the rooms could end up being a much bigger venture than we imagined.

The Party in the Park event was happening at the weekend so we decided to spend the afternoon watching the bands and promoting Backbeat. The set-up was pretty good but the event was seriously lacking a beer tent. Apparently this was because people are terrified of young people drinking and rioting but I can't understand why these things can't be controlled.

The event confirmed to us that there are a lot of talented bands around and I was given the opportunity to get up on stage and talk about Backbeat. The disappointing thing was that none of the bands approached us or took any of the flyers we had left around the place and unfortunately this was a sign of things to come.

## A SUMMER VISITOR

The summer weather was beginning to kick in now and so walks with the dogs on the beach and bike rides became our aims on the rare weekends we had off work. The lifestyle we were looking for definitely became more apparent with the warmer weather and when the sun shone even some of the business pressure seemed to fade away.

Julie's mum was due to arrive for a visit and so we were quite excited about finally having a relative over here to share our life with. The plan was for all of us to drive to Auckland to meet Julie's mum at the airport, but work had been slow and so I had to accept a job in Rotorua. This meant Julie and Sam taking the drive up on their own. Julie had never driven to Auckland before and did OK until she came up against some of New Zealand's strange ideas on road signs. A sign will appear directing you to the airport, but then there will be no more signs and you will come up to a junction and wonder which direction to go in. I forgot to tell Julie about this and I had kept the map of Auckland at home. They did eventually arrive back safely and the flight hadn't been too hard on Julie's mum.

She was very jet-lagged and emotional, especially at seeing the children. It was weird because, even though it had been so long since we had seen her (11 months), it seemed like only yesterday. I guess this is how you eventually get over the homesickness, as time is a great healer and when relatives do come to visit, the world really does seem a small place.

Unfortunately, Daryl (Julie's mum) had arrived at a very stressful time for us, with the rooms not being as busy as we had hoped. Things were pretty tense and Julie and I were both at the point where we were seriously considering packing up our dreams and going back to the UK. So wanting to show Darryl what a wonderful place we had moved to was sort of pushed to the back of our minds.

I have slowly learnt to deal with stress by blanking it out. I don't know if this is the right thing to do, and a pyschiatrist may say it is actually a bad thing to do but it seems to work for me. I had, however, started to wake up with a horrible feeling of dread every morning and was constantly asking myself 'What have I done?'.

Julie and I have had lots of chats about our life here and although we have major worries we believe that if you work hard you will be rewarded. We decided to carry on pushing Backbeat but if it got to a point where it was going to start eating into the small amount of savings that were left then we would have to pull out.

Having Daryl around helped to take our minds off things and we decided to take a drive to Maclaren Falls, which is about a 20 minute drive from Tauranga. It was a beautiful sunny day and as we had never been to the falls before we really didn't know what to expect. There is a park around the falls with a farmyard and café. We walked through a tropical forest and saw a small waterfall hidden away in the trees.

It is really important to take the time to visit places like this and, with a lot of natural attractions in New Zealand not charging an entrance fee, it is a very cheap day out. I remember when we had time off work in Coventry we would end up going to Birmingham or Stratford upon Avon and would usually end up spending a fortune in the shops or restaurants. Zoë and Sam got to play with a lamb and we all relaxed and enjoyed the stunning scenery. One of the good things about living in a new country is that you always stumble across new places and every day really does throw up a new opportunity. If we ever did move away from New Zealand then the scenery is something we would definitely miss.

The fine weather made up our minds to finally go and buy a barbeque. We had been here 11 months and had yet to enjoy this piece of Kiwiana. Most people here have gas powered barbeques and the range on offer is amazing. Julie went for something called the Kiwi Backyard, which is a basic three burner but fine for what we need.  I arrived home from work and they had all planned for us to have a barbeque, so with only an hour before I had to be at Backbeat I went about setting up the barbeque, helped by a couple of cold bottles of Tui (lager).

We had steak sandwiches and as I sat there in the sunshine I wondered if Backbeat was the right thing for us to do, as it would be eating into valuble family times like this. We need the money, though, so off I went, leaving Julie and her mum to do the cleaning up. Having Daryl around was also making me miss my parents even more and in phone conversations with them lately I had been finding it hard not to break down with all the pressure we were under.

I decided to have a chat with Jason, our landlord at the unit, to tell him of the predicament we were in regarding the rooms. I explained that although we were trying everything we could, the bands just didn't seem to be interested at the moment and this would mean us paying the rent out of our own money which was something we couldn't afford to do. I also said that if we didn't manage to get more bands into Backbeat then we wouldn't be able to sign a lease (Jason had been kind enough not to make us sign one immediately). Jason said he had every faith in us, which was reassuring, but not much faith in the bands, so we agreed to keep in touch and to keep working at it.

The weeks passed by and with it being summer a lot of the bands were taking holidays, so we were actually getting cancellations from regular bands as well as no interest from new bands. The pressure was becoming unbearable and after a lot of soul searching we decided that even with the help from the Youth Trust and Tauranga council we couldn't see Backbeat NZ attracting anywhere near the amount of bands we needed to make an income.

We had two options: walk away from the business and lose the money we had put in or try to sell it as a good idea to somebody who was in a stronger financial position than us. It was around this time that I hit an all time low emotionally, as for the first time in my life I felt that I was failing. I was failing to provide a decent income and now the one business I knew I could make work obviously wasn't going to succeed as I had planned. The other dilemma was how to find somebody willing to take on the business when it wasn't covering the rent – and if we couldn't make it work, then who could? When things are bad we just keep soldiering on until they improve, but another bombshell was about to drop...

## BAD NEWS

Daryl received a phone call saying that her dad was going to hospital for some tests. I won't go into too many details but Daryl was very upset and decided she needed to go back to the UK to see her dad. I then received a phone call from my parents telling me that my grandad had been taken into hospital and that things didn't look very good.

On top of all the business worries, we now felt we needed to be with our families in the UK. Eventually we decided to approach the bank to see if we could borrow some money to get back for a few weeks to see our grandparents. We did have the return part of the tickets the BBC bought us, so this would reduce the cost of the flights.

The morning Daryl's coach arrived to take her to the airport was very upsetting. She had planned to spend Christmas with us and although she had been here a few weeks it only seemed like yesterday that she arrived. There were a lot of tears and the feeling of isolation from friends and family was back again. In hindsight, it hadn't been the best time to visit us with all the pressure we were under, and we looked forward to a time when we were more settled and Daryl could visit again.

I would say that if you do make the move to New Zealand then try to put off relatives from visiting in the first year and resist the urge to re-visit the UK for as long as possible.

We only had a short time to use the return part of our original tickets so we were planning to fly out on Christmas or Boxing Day! However, finances were not looking good and we didn't have a buyer for the rooms. The bank advised us that they probably could lend us the money but without the rooms being sold all we could see was us being in a worse financial position when we returned.

The need to pay a visit to the UK was very strong but it was obvious that we could put ourselves in a very difficult financial position if we did go. We decided that without a buyer for the rooms we couldn't make the journey. It was a horrible feeling and this was all happening during our first Christmas away from family. We were told that your first Christmas in New Zealand can be one of the hardest times anyway, so we desperately needed some good news.

In the same way we had received the calls within days of each other of our grandparents being ill we then received news that their health was improving. This was great news but the stress we were under had taken its toll. I was seriously considering packing everything in and going back to the UK. Car Care was doing well, so we knew we could sell it for a profit, and with the money we had made on the house we could return to the UK without losing any of the money we had invested in making the move to New Zealand.

I was still feeling very bitter about the failure of the rehearsal rooms and the fact that we didn't have the finances to support them staying open through the first difficult months. You see I still believed they were a good idea and maybe we just hadn't given the business enough time to establish itself. The bands continued to ignore our advertising, though, which meant we had no choice but to set ourselves the deadline of the end of January to either sell Backbeat or walk away, losing a lot of time and money.

The stress was putting a huge strain on us as a family – especially Julie and me – so we decided we needed a short break to take our minds off everything. We found a cheap motel in Wellington which allowed us to take the dogs and booked in for three nights starting on Boxing Day.

## A MUCH-NEEDED BREAK

We chose Wellington for lots of reasons (capital city, lots to do, etc.) but the main thing I needed was to rediscover why we had moved out here I felt the six-hour drive through the North Island would help us do this. It's amazing what a tonic a few days' break can be and once we had booked the motel some of our pressures seemed to lift. The drive from Tauranga to Wellington was amazing, as we hadn't been further south than Rotorua and we were finally going to see places we had heard so much about such as Taupo and the Desert Road.

Lake Taupo is mind blowing in it's size (around the same size as Singapore) but when you add the fact that it is a volcanic crater words fail to describe the feeling when you are driving around the edge of it. We had a short stop in Taupo for some breakfast and it seems to be a very nice place. The lake front is lined with motels, hotels and restaurants and the town centre, although small, has a character and charm that adds to the relaxing feeling you get looking out over the crystal clear blue water.

After our brief stop in Taupo we headed south along what is known as the 'Desert Road'. The road takes you alongside Mount Ruapehu, one of the North Islands most breath-taking mountains – which also happens to be an active volcano. The reason behind the road's name (it is actually State Highway 1) soon becomes apparent as after some amazingly sharp bends, the road straightens and the scenery changes from lush greenery to barren scrubland. You can imagine in years gone by a huge volcanic eruptions wiping out all forms of life around here. Now long grass, which makes the land look like it has grown hair, whips around in the wind making the earth appear to be moving.

The New Zealand army do a lot of their training here and it also seems to be popular with motor cross riders and four-wheel-drive enthusiasts. Sights like these were beginning to lighten my mood and strengthen my belief that New Zealand has a lot more in store for us. Making a move like this is an adventure and it was now becoming apparent that a different lifestyle can be within reach, even without having a pile of money.

As we drew closer to Wellington the heavens opened and rain poured down, making the treacherous New Zealand roads even more heart-stopping. Wellington is known as the windy city and the weather can be quite changeable so the rain wasn't a surprise. When we stepped out of the car to enter our motel, though, the wind nearly blew us off our feet! Julie started to unload the car while I checked in. The girl at the counter was British and recognised me immediately. It turned out she had met up with some backpackers who were staying just down the road from us and they had come from Coventry. They say the world is a small place but in New Zealand it does sometimes feel that everybody knows one another.

We were pretty tired after the six-hour drive from Tauranga so we decided to have an early night and explore Wellington the following morning. After again nearly getting blown off my feet taking the dogs for an early morning walk, we headed into Wellington on the local train. Sam loved the journey and it reminded me that despite its size Tauranga really needs better public transport. I was surprised at how compact Wellington town centre is, but it also has some stunning views and the city is clean and well laid out. There was a more cosmopolitan feel walking around and of course Julie loved the variety of shops.

We had a great day just taking our time and discovering new places and I could see why Wellington has often been voted as one of the most desirable cities in the world in which to live. However, there were some things that I was about to find out that would make me think twice about living in Wellington.

Te Papa is an amazing museum based in Wellington and one of the most amazing things about it is its free admission policy. It is by far the best museum I have been in and if you are ever in Wellington then make sure you give it a visit. It was during our visit here that I discovered, amongst other things, how earthquakes can affect New Zealand and especially Wellington. There is a plaque on the wall at Te Papa overlooking the harbour and hills in the distance. The words on this plaque explain how the hills you are looking at were formed during enormous earthquakes and that the next one could strike at any time.

I looked up at the houses perched on these hills, their foundations balanced on wooden stilts and imagined the whole lot tumbling down into the sea. Now I know the whole of New

Zealand is prone to earthquakes. In fact, we have one everyday, although most go unnoticed. Tauranga is especially susceptible to an Earthquake-induced tsunami, but a city built on a fault line is just a little too close for comfort for me.

The short break was having a great effect on all of us and we were beginning to feel more positive about things. A lot of the pressures you go through when emigrating to New Zealand can be lifted by simply changing your perspective on things. You have to try to look at the positive side in everything and believe that things will get better. For us our homesickness was disappearing, which meant we could focus on our future in New Zealand rather than running back home to the UK.

We also had two phone calls the following morning that would mark another turning point in our journey. Eugene from Bay City Music called to say he had found a buyer for the Backbeat rehearsal rooms and an hour or so later so did our friend Karl. Just as we were thinking nobody would want to buy the business, we were about to receive two offers. The sun was shining and we had another relaxing day in Wellington, finished off with a meal in a beachside restaurant. These are the sort of times we would miss if we did end our New Zealand adventure and there are probably more of them than we realise.

## A SPECIAL NEW YEAR

Upon our return I phoned Eugene and said I would see him after New Year about the buyer for the rooms and Karl turned out to be on tour with his band in the South Island so I wouldn't be able to see him until his return on the 15th of January. The weather was glorious on New Year's Eve but we really didn't know what to do. With two dogs, two kids and no babysitter, a night in with a DVD was looking quite a certainty.

Late that afternoon we decided to visit our friends Rick and Chris to see what they were up to. We were sitting on their balcony overlooking the Mount drinking a beer and looking at photos of their journey around New Zealand when Julie came up with the idea of going camping for the night.

The camp sites around Tauranga and the surrounding area at this time of year and especially New Year's Eve are always fully booked, plus we had two dogs. But to my surprise, after a few calls we found a site with a couple of places left that was willing to allow us to bring the dogs as well. We finished our drinks and shot off to the supermarket to buy some disposable barbeques, drinks, etc. and headed down to Little Waihi, which is about 30 kilometres from Tauranga.

The campsite is situated directly on the beach and the owners were putting on a karaoke show and bonfire for everyone to enjoy. After the tents were up I took the kids body boarding, then we came back and settled in for the night. We sat there around the barbeque and had one of the best New Years I've ever had. Sitting around the beach bonfire looking at the clear sky at midnight really is my ideal way of spending New Year. The feeling that things were going to improve for us was getting stronger.

I've never really been one for New Years resolutions but on New Years day Julie and I took the kids for a walk up Mount

Maunganui. We talked about our plans for the future and decided that if we successfully sold the rehearsal rooms we would use the money to pay our mortgage for one year or until we could comfortably use the money from Car Care. At the end of the year we would review our position and look at our options, such as selling the business and getting a job, as we would then have permanent residence, or even possibly moving to another town. If the Car Care business were to grow as it had in its first year, then the prospects of expanding it were very real. I guess what we were saying is that come January 2005 we would have more options and more choices to make, but the one thing we did decide was that we no longer wanted to return to the UK.

We sold the rehearsal rooms four weeks later to Eugene from Bay Music. Although it was tinged with sadness and frustration it was the best thing to do and took away the pressure we had been under since opening them. We also realised that in my effort to earn money I had probably spread myself too thinly and that could have been why things hadn't worked out as we had planned.

In the year since we had arrived I had tried to earn money by singing, writing, promoting bands and setting up the rehearsal studio as well as running Car Care. In hindsight, I had panicked thinking that Car Care would never make us enough to live comfortably and I would come to Julie nearly every month with a new money-making scheme. What I should have done is just relax and let the business grow naturally.

Julie has a great knack of bringing me down to earth and she spelled it out to me that we should concentrate on Car Care and making a life for ourselves here. We came out here to enjoy the lifestyle and I was re-creating the long hours of work we had come to get away from. I have recently been given the opportunity to promote bands at Tauranga's main music venue and as music is in our blood Julie and I are going to do this together. It is only one night per week and it could give us the opportunity to finally make some Kiwi friends.

## OUR NEW LIFE – FINANCIAL TRUTHS

Well, we have spent a year in New Zealand and have survived through some very difficult times. I will say that most of our problems have been due to financial pressure from the house not selling as quickly as we expected in the UK.

There are a few other things which we hadn't found out about in our research prior to making the move here, such as paying tax on every dollar earned. Unlike in the UK there is no lower earnings threshold in the NZ tax system, i.e. you can't earn say $10,000 dollars each before you start to pay tax. In addition, you only need to earn just over $38,000 per year before you go from the 19 per cent to the 33 per cent tax level.

The cost of living here is about the same as in the UK when you factor in the lower Kiwi wage. For instance, in our current situation we have a mortgage of $240,000, which works out at around $1,400 per month on an interest-only mortgage, which we chose while the business is growing. Once we start to earn more money the plan is to pay off more of the mortgage. Food for four of us works out at around $180 per week and we spend $90 per week on petrol as we do a lot of driving for the business.

This all means that I currently need to earn around $1000 per week after tax to enjoy the sort of lifestyle we came here for.

We have made mistakes, and setting up the rehearsal studio was a massive risk as we didn't have the back-up money to sustain the business if response was slow. The pressure has been taken away by using the money spent setting up the studio to pay the mortgage for a year and waiting for the Car Care business to grow. I only wish we had thought of that option sooner.

Some people would say that the house we bought is the main problem, as we still have a big mortgage. However, because of the property boom in Tauranga our house is currently valued at around $400,000, so we have made a massive $100,000 in under a year and prices are still rising!

When you first look at New Zealand it does seem like paradise and there is no denying that it is a beautiful place to live in. You can, however, feel very isolated and it is very difficult to adjust to the drop in income you will probably have to take when moving from the UK. For example, a meal in a resturant out here will cost around $60 for the four of us, which is only about £20 but when you consider that $60 is a day's wage for a lot of people here then it puts the cost of living into perspective.

When you first arrive it is very difficult to stop converting prices back into UK pounds, but you should try to stop this as soon as possible otherwise things will seem a lot less expensive than they actually are.

## MISSING THE SOCIAL LIFE

Missing friends has been one of the hardest things for us to cope
with. Something as simple as a good night out with your mates,
which you take for granted in your home town, feels like a very
distant memory. We used to organise coach trips to Rock City in
Nottingham for all the bands at the rehearsal studio, so 52 of us
would pile into a coach and have a great time. Even if I had 52
friends over here there isn't anywhere like Rock City for us to go
to (although Hamilton looks promising).

I think of nights we used to spend in the rehearsal rooms sitting
around chatting with mates or Julie and I driving down to
London to check out a band or go shopping. We miss all that,
and we would need a serious amount of money just to hop over
'the ditch' to Australia to see a band, let alone flying back to the
UK. Which leads me to our next problem.

Before we moved out here we envisaged travelling back to the
UK every other year or so for a holiday and to visit relatives. At
the moment I can't see us being able to afford a holiday in New
Zealand, let alone flying back to the UK. So I guess I am making
the point that money is tight for us here, but money isn't
everything and there is another saying which makes sense to me
now: 'What doesn't kill you makes you stronger'.

We have made a lot of friends here who moved from the UK
recently. It has been interesting finding out their reasons for
making the move, which on the whole seem to be similar to ours.
There is a feeling that the UK is overcrowded and the cost of
living is escalating but the main reason for choosing New

Zealand seems to be the chance to create a more diverse and safer lifestyle for our children. As far as I can tell, the people we have met would all agree that their kids love it here and although the education system is slightly different I haven't heard any complaints about the standard of schooling.

Our children are thriving and Zoë loves coming home and telling us new facts she has found out about our new home. She already has a strong network of friends and even Sam – who is only four – has his friends round for tea. The beach lifestyle suits the children and I do plan to take up surfing this summer! The relaxed lifestyle can be a bit frustrating, though, especially when I am driving along the beachfront to my next job on a sunny summer afternoon and all I can see is people having 'barbies' or relaxing on the beach.

We are one year into our journey now and although things are improving and the outlook is promising the move was still a lot more difficult than we expected it to be. Some people might wonder what I am moaning about, especially if you saw *Get a new life* and the beautiful shots of Tauranga used in the programme.

Making a move like this is an adventure and you will face the unexpected and be in a constant state of re-evaluation. You will need to compromise and be flexible, but finally if it is really what you want then you will settle. You probably want to know if I think moving here was the right thing to do or if we plan on staying? Well I'll begin to answer these questions by re-capping on the reasons we moved here.

## WHY STAY IN NEW ZEALAND?

### Friendly People

On the whole I would say this has been the case. There is definitely less aggression here, which is probably due to the more relaxed lifestyle and the fact that the place doesn't feel crowded – except when you are trying to drive over the harbour bridge in Tauranga in rush hour! New Zealanders do have a very different culture to us Brits, though and you will notice very subtle differences which can emphasise the feeling of being an outsider. There is also a bit of what I would call 'small town mentality' which can be frustrating. However, this is probably because Tauranga was and still is a very small city by UK standards and it is having to cope with 150 new people settling every day.

The Kiwi sense of humour will also take a bit of getting used – to or maybe it's that the Kiwis have trouble getting used to our witty ways. People here on the whole are friendlier and I have met strangers who will do almost anything to make you feel welcome.

### Low Crime Rate

Luckily we haven't been affected by crime yet and we don't know anybody who has. And yes, some people do still leave their cars and houses unlocked when they go out. People will be people, though, and New Zealand has its own issues with youth crime and drugs like does every other country in the world. But the newspapers are notoriously thin on crime stories, which I guess this is a good measure of where the New Zealand crime rate is at. At the end of the day we can all look at the latest crime figures, but the question is: do we feel safer here? The answer has got to be yes.

### Good for the Children

As I have mentioned, we feel New Zealand is still a good place to bring up children. However, I would also strongly encourage my kids to travel to other countries as soon as they are old enough, because New Zealand does tend to shelter you from the rest of the world. This is great when you are slowing down but is also probably why such a high per centage of 18 – 25-year-olds do the big overseas experience. Staying here long enough to get citizenship is still one of our aims so that our children will have the choice of living in New Zealand, Australia or the UK.

### The Lifestyle

This was probably the reason at the top of our list for wanting to come here. We needed to get away from the rat race. Tauranga is a beautiful place and is one of the few places that lives up to its sunshine paradise title. Living in a great house by the beach and enjoying the cafes and bars and watersports that are all around us would be fantastic, but the reality for us is that we haven't enjoyed the lifestyle yet.

We haven't seen much of the country yet, apart from Christchurch, Auckland and Tauranga, but we do plan to rectify this as soon as we can. There are definitely aspects of the lifestyle here that we would miss if we chose to move back to the UK, such as the beach, BBQ bacon for breakfast, and the open spaces. On the other hand, the relaxed lifestyle has also been a bit of a hindrance when getting our businesses off the ground. People here tend not to rush into anything (whereas we do) and so everything just takes that little bit longer to happen.

We also miss the buzz of living in a big city and the UK nightlife. I would say the lifestyle is one of the main reasons that Brits look at New Zealand, but the funny thing is I would say it takes around a year of living here to finally understand what the lifestyle is and to get used to it.

## AND FINALLY...

One year into the move to New Zealand we have finally made the descision that we are not planning on returning to the UK. Things are looking more positive for us and Car Care is doing really well, to the point where hopefully this year I will either employ someone or set up a second van. Julie is planning to find some part-time work once Sam starts school and Zoë is doing well in her studies.

It has been the right move for us to make and even with the mistakes we have made I believe we are a stronger and closer family. We have set ourselves the target of one year from now to achieve our goal of putting ourselves in a stronger financial position and come January 2005 we will review our situation with the increased options permanent residence would give us.

Hopefully this book has shown that, although emigrating isn't an easy thing to do – even for people like us who were 100% certain about the move – if you persevere and are a strong family unit the rewards are there to be had. A move like this isn't for everyone and I know of people who have tried it and ended up with broken relationships and financial ruin.

My advice would be to think hard about your reasons for making the move and look at all the options. It could be that a move within the UK may actually be all you need for that fresh start that most of us look for at some point in our life.

We are finally beginning to feel settled in New Zealand, but we don't expect it to be a bed of roses. One thing I have found that has helped recently is to not think of the move here as a final chapter in your life. I feel a lot of people make a move like this because they feel trapped in the life they have built for themselves. If you don't see your situation as necessarily permanent then it becomes an adventure and the feeling that there could be something new on the horizon begins to drive you.

We are living year by year and setting our goals that way. After all, you only live once, so even if you do move to New Zealand keep your options open and live life to the full.

*Hare Mae*
The Goddards

# Useful Contacts

I do not know how people researched a move like ours prior to the invention of the world wide web. Use a search engine such as 'Google' and you can find almost anything you need to know. The five websites I have listed I used constantly in my research. The other companies I have listed I can personally recommend for their service and support. Note the New Zealand phone numbers have the 00 64 dialing code in front of them to be used when dialing from the UK.

**New Zealand Immigration**
www.immigration.govt.nz

**UK Emigration sites**
www.uk2nz.co.uk
www.britishexpats.com

**The Emigration Group**
www.emigration.uk.com

**Tauranga website**
www.citynews.co.nz

**John Mason International Movers (removal company)**
35 Wilson Road, Liverpool, Merseyside L36 6AE
Tel: 0151 449 3938
www.johnmason.com

**The Emigration Group (emigration consultants)**
7 Heritage Court, Lower Bridge Street, Chester CH1 1RD
Tel: 01244 321414
www.emigration.uk.com

**Car Care NZ**
PO Box 59042, Mangere Bridge, Auckland 1730
Tel: 00 64 9 634 7708
Email: nz@carcare.co.nz
www.carcare.co.nz

**Rent a Dent / First Choice Car Rentals**
Excellent car rental company throughout NZ and also at Auckland
Airport.
Tel: 00 64 9 275 2044
Email: aucklandairport@rentadent.co.nz
www.rentadent.co.nz

**Business Networking Institute (B.N.I.)**
If you are setting up a business then join the local chapter of the
B.N.I. – it really works!!!
www.bni.co.nz

**Golden Arrow Shippers (for shipping pets to NZ)**
Lydbury North, Shropshire SY7 8AY
Tel: 01588 680240

**For People Looking At Moving To Tauranga**

## Tony Hammond Motors

Provides excellent service the place we bought our car.

1198 Cameron Road, Tauranga

Tel: 00 64 7 578 5488

Email: thammomd@xtra.co.nz

## The Importer

We had so many nice comments about our furniture. This is where we bought most of it.

Grey Street, Tauranga

Tel: 00 64 7 571 8103

## The Furniture and Bedroom Warehouse

This is the place we bought the rest of our furniture.

353 Cameron Road, Tauranga

Tel: 00 64 7 579 0555

## Priority One

This agency help people who are setting up a new business in the Bay.

29 Grey Street, Tauranga

Tel: 00 64 7 571 1401

## 11th Avenue Motel

Quality motel! Great location. This is at Memorial park where the film crew stayed.

26 Eleventh Ave, Tauranga

Tel: 00 64 7 577 1881

**St Mary's Tahatai Centre**
Sam's nursery school near our house in Papamoa.
114 Evans Road, Papamoa, Tauranga
Tel: 00 64 7 572 5016

**Mount Maunganui Primary School**
Zoë's school in a great location near Mount Beach.
Orkney Road, Mount Maunganui
Tel: 00 64 7 575 3960

**Papamoa Kennels and Cattery**
Our dogs get groomed and stay here.
Welcome Bay Road, Papamoa, Tauranga
Tel: 00 64 7 542 0730

# Vivien Edwards - Photgrapher

Like the Goddards, Vivien Edwards was born in England and came to live in New Zealand with her family when aged five years.

Her book about the life and work of the photographer Henry Winkelmann (1860-1931): *Winkelmann: Images of Early New Zealand*, published by Benton Ross 1987 was a winner in the 1988 New Zealand Book of the Year Awards.

Inspired by Winkelmann, who left a legacy of more than 10,000 glass-plate negatives to the Auckland Institute and Museum, Vivien began taking photographs for her own interest, and also to illustrate articles she was writing for trade and professional magazines.

Vivien regards New Zealand as a photographer's paradise.

'Not only is the scenery stunning, but one doesn't need to travel far to find a completely different environment in which to take pictures. From where I live in Te Puna, just outside Tauranga, in the Bay of Plenty, it takes about three and a half hours from lying on a sunny beach, to snow skiing on a central North Island mountain.'

Working with the Te Puna Heartland community group, she recently took photographs and designed a brochure on Te Puna, which has now been reprinted.

For writing and photographic assignments, Vivien can be contacted at 16 Perkins Drive, Te Puna, RD 6, Tauranga, NZ Ph 00-64-07-552-4437 Fax 00-64-07-552-6663 or words-pics@wave.co.nz

**If you want to know how...**

♦ To buy a home in the sun, and let it out
♦ To move overseas, and work well with the people who live there
♦ To get the job you want, in the career you like
♦ To plan a wedding, and make the Best Man's speech
♦ To build your own home, or manage a conversion
♦ To buy and sell houses, and make money from doing so
♦ To gain new skills and learning, at a later time in life
♦ To empower yourself, and improve your lifestyle
♦ To start your own business, and run it profitably
♦ To prepare for your retirement, and generate a pension
♦ To improve your English, or write a PhD
♦ To be a more effective manager, and a good communicator
♦ To write a book, and get it published

If you want to know how to do all these things
and much, much more...

**howto**books

## If you want to know how...

to emigrate to New Zealand and make a new life there

'Many visitors become so impressed with their initial visits to New Zealand and what it has to offer that they decide they want to live there. So how can you find out about all those things you need to know about starting a new life in a new country? Where can you go to find out about the history of New Zealand, schools, housing, employment opportunities, setting up in business, paying taxes and an overview of both immigration and general law?

This little handbook is a real beaut! It's packed full of easily accessible bits of information that you need to know about getting set up and starting to live in New Zealand.'

Matthew Collins and Mary Nelson

### GOING TO LIVE IN NEW ZEALAND

**Matthew Collins and Mary Nelson**

Moving to the other side of the world is a huge step, but this new book takes much of the hard work out of relocating to New Zealand. It is full of information on the latest immigration policies to identify what category may work best for you, plus all you need to know about housing, taxes and healthcare. It even covers how best to ship your property and pets to your new home, and the best places to visit once you're there.

ISBN 1 85703 965 3

## If you want to know how...

to find work and enjoy life in New Zealand

'I hope my book, based on 23 years' first-hand experience, will be some help to you in planning your stay in New Zealand – and who knows – perhaps making a whole new life here as many have before.'

Joy Muirhead

## LIVING AND WORKING IN NEW ZEALAND

**Joy Muirhead**

'The definitive guide to setting up a new life in the other Down Under.' – Overseas Jobs Express

'...takes you by the hand and leads you through the confusing maze of immigration categories and visa applications... And once you're there, the book tells you how to earn a dollar, what gummies, dummies and chooks are and whether you're likely to encounter avalanches (and what to do if you do!).' – Destination New Zealand

ISBN 1 85703 912 2

How To Books are available through all good bookshops, or you can order direct from us through Grantham Book Services.

Tel: +44 (0)1476 541080
Fax: +44 (0)1476 541061
Email: orders@gbs.tbs-ltd.co.uk

Or via our web site www.howtobooks.co.uk

To order via any of these methods please quote the title(s) of the book(s) and your credit card number together with its expiry date.

For further information about our books and catalogue, please contact:

How To Books
3 Newtec Place
Magdalen Road
Oxford OX4 1RE

Visit our website at www.howtobooks.co.uk

Or you can contact us by email at info@howtobooks.co.uk